Dedication

To Susanne Doell, Ph.D., culturally sensitive therapist, spouse, colleague, and soul mate.

PSYCHOLOGY PRACTITIONER GUIDEBOOKS

EDITORS

Arnold P. Goldstein, Syracuse University
Leonard Krasner, Stanford University & SUNY at Stony Brook
Sol L. Garfield, Washington University in St. Louis

PSYCHOTHERAPY AND COUNSELING WITH MINORITIES

Pergamon Titles of Related Interest

Higginbotham/West/Forsyth PSYCHOTHERAPY AND BEHAVIOR
CHANGE: Social, Cultural and Methodological Perspectives
Jenkins THE PSYCHOLOGY OF THE AFRO-AMERICAN:
A Humanistic Approach
Segall/Dasen/Berry/Poortinga HUMAN BEHAVIOR IN GLOBAL
PERSPECTIVE: An Introduction to Cross-Cultural Psychology
Snyder/Forsyth HANDBOOK OF SOCIAL AND CLINICAL
PSYCHOLOGY: The Health Perspective

Related Journals
(Free sample copies available upon request)

CLINICAL PSYCHOLOGY REVIEW
INTERNATIONAL JOURNAL OF INTERCULTURAL RELATIONS
THE ARTS IN PSYCHOTHERAPY

PSYCHOTHERAPY AND COUNSELING WITH MINORITIES

A Cognitive Approach to Individual and Cultural Differences

MANUEL RAMIREZ III

University of Texas at Austin

PERGAMON PRESS

Member of Maxwell Macmillan Pergamon Publishing Corporation

New York • Oxford • Beijing • Frankfurt

São Paulo • Sydney • Tokyo • Toronto

Pergamon Press Offices:

U.S.A.	Pergamon Press, Inc., Maxwell House, Fairview Park, Elmsford, New York 10523, U.S.A.
U.K.	Pergamon Press plc, Headington Hill Hall, Oxford OX3 0BW, England
PEOPLE'S REPUBLIC OF CHINA	Pergamon Press, Xizhimenwai Dajie, Beijing Exhibition Centre, Beijing 100044, People's Republic of China
FEDERAL REPUBLIC OF GERMANY	Pergamon Press GmbH, Hammerweg 6, D-6242 Kronberg, Federal Republic of Germany
BRAZIL	Pergamon Editora Ltda, Rua Eça de Queiros, 346, CEP 04011, Paraiso, São Paulo, Brazil
AUSTRALIA	Pergamon Press Australia Pty Ltd., P.O. Box 544, Potts Point, NSW 2011, Australia
JAPAN	Pergamon Press, 8th Floor, Matsuoka Central Building, 1-7-1 Nishishinjuku, Shinjuku-ku, Tokyo 160, Japan
CANADA	Pergamon Press Canada Ltd., Suite 271, 253 College Street, Toronto, Ontario M5T 1R5, Canada

---

Copyright © 1991 Pergamon Press, Inc.

Library of Congress Cataloging in Publication Data

Ramirez, Michael, 1937-
    Psychotherapy and counseling with minorities : a cognitive
approach to individual and cultural differences / by Manuel Ramirez
III.
      p. cm. -- (Psychology practitioner guidebooks)
    Includes index.
    ISBN 0-08-036443-8 (hardcover : alk. paper) :
    ISBN 0-08-036442-X (pbk. : alk. paper)
    1. Minorities--Mental health. 2. Minorities--Counseling of.
3. Psychotherapy--Cross-cultural studies. 4. Cross-cultural
counseling.   I. Title. II. Series.
    [DNLM: 1. Counseling--methods. 2. Cross-Cultural Comparison.
3. Minority Groups--psychology. 4. Psychotherapy--methods. WM 420
R173p]
    RC451.5.A2R36 1991
    616.89'14--dc20
    DNLM/DLC
    for Library of Congress   90-7784
                                            CIP

Printing: 1 2 3 4 5 6 7 8 9   Year: 1 2 3 4 5 6 7 8 9 0

Contents

Preface

This book is the culmination of my twenty-five years of experience in research and implementation work in public education, university, community, and clinical settings. My work has centered on the experiences of "the different"—those who, in some way, do not fit the preferred or idealized images of society; those who, because of their uniqueness, are subject to pressures to conform, prejudice, and oppression.

I began my work in this area thinking that only members of ethnic and racial minority groups suffered from the marginality syndrome resulting from feeling different. Through research and intervention work with people from all ethnic, religious, and socioeconomic backgrounds, I have come to realize that the mismatch syndrome is common to most people who live and work in diverse societies.

As I developed and implemented educational programs in schools, taught courses, lectured at different colleges and universities, and worked with clients in psychotherapy and counseling, I came to realize that no one fits their society's idealized images perfectly.

For some, the lack of fit was due to external features—skin color, accent, physical appearance, or impairments. For others, the lack of fit was due to internal, or "invisible" characteristics—values, thinking style, emotional and expressive style, or sexual preference.

My work with the different gradually led me to the realization that traditional approaches to education, psychotherapy, and counseling were not adequate or appropriate for intervention; what was needed was a new theoretical and research perspective, and a new model of personality change.

This book introduces a model of psychotherapy and counseling based on the multicultural perspective that evolved from my work with the different. The model is presented in the context of four case histories—

an adolescent Hispanic woman, a middle-aged mainstream Anglo man, a male African-American adolescent, and a middle-aged mainstream Anglo woman.

The principal objectives of the model are to help people who feel different and alienated to accept and understand their uniqueness. The model also seeks to develop cultural (values) and coping (cognitive styles) flexibility.

There are five characteristics of a multicultural orientation to life:

The first of these characteristics is the striving for the maximum development of the personality; a striving for self-actualization.

People with a multicultural orientation to life are motivated to develop as many aspects of their personality as possible. Multicultural people recognize that interacting with diversity can stimulate the evolution of undeveloped areas of the personality. The multiculturally oriented recognize that stereotypes, and notions of societal, cultural, and personality superiority or inferiority can block experience and learning filters, preventing them from valuing people, groups, and cultures who might otherwise act as teachers and catalysts for development.

Culturally flexible people are willing to take diversity challenges; to risk situations totally unlike previous experiences. Such individuals learn by observation, by listening, and by exposure to new world views and different life philosophies.

A second characteristic of multicultural orientation is adaptability to different environmental situations. Regardless of how work, educational, or other environmental conditions change, multicultural people are motivated to adapt and to flex in order to be effective.

Thirdly, the person with a multicultural orientation enjoys the challenges of leadership roles in diverse groups. He or she evolves innovative solutions in resolving conflict in groups with diverse memberships (Ramirez, 1983; Garza et al., 1982).

Another characteristic is the multicultural person's commitment to changing groups, cultures, and nations to guarantee social justice for all members and citizens. Such a person has a goal of helping to develop a perfect society. Although multicultural people may feel more comfortable in their native group, they develop perspectives as world citizens (Ramirez, 1983).

Adler observed that multicultural people can transcend families, groups, and cultures (1974); that is, they have the ability to step back in order to take an objective look at the groups with which they are familiar, and in which they have participated to determine what has to be modified to ensure social justice and equity for all members.

The final characteristic of people with a multicultural orientation to life is motivation to get the most out of life. Multicultural people seek exposure to as much diversity in life as possible. They enjoy traveling and living in different environments such as different countries, different regions of the same country, or different areas within their communities. They enjoy meeting different people, whether in person or through biographies and autobiographies.

But, how does the Multicultural Model fit into the overall psychotherapy and counseling picture? Do counselors and therapists need to make major changes in the way they do therapy in order to be effective as multicultural therapists?

The techniques and strategies of the Multicultural Model reflect an eclecticism, ranging from the intensive study of the client's life history and the use of insight, to the employment of cognitive behaviorial approaches. Multicultural therapy is unique, however, in its theoretical concepts and goals of change.

The Multicultural Model of psychotherapy and counseling is eclectic with respect to techniques and strategies. From the dynamic approaches and theories of therapy, the Multicultural Model has borrowed a focus on collecting a detailed life history. This life history helps the therapist or counselor understand the client's past and develop insight for making the unconscious conscious through interpretations.

From the humanistic perspective, the Multicultural Model borrows unconditional positive regard, that is, uncritical acceptance, to allow a client to accept his or her unique self. Also from the humanistic approach comes the use of phenomenology, or the therapist's attempt to see the world through the eyes of the client.

From the cognitive and behavioristic approaches and theories, the Multicultural Model places an emphasis on stress reduction, on establishing behavioral goals, and on emphasizing homework and the client's active participation through role-playing.

Finally, from the cross-cultural, ethnopsychological, and community schools, the Multicultural Model has adopted an emphasis on values and on the assumption that each cultural and environmental set of circumstances or conditions produces a unique set of coping techniques, or cognitive styles, crucial to personality development and functioning.

The theoretical base of the Multicultural Model of psychotherapy and counseling has its origins in cross-cultural mental health, and in the psychology of liberation that evolved from developments in the psychologies of ethnic minorities, the colonized, and women. The cross-cultural emphasis evolved from the application of psychoanalytic and behavioristic theories and intervention approaches in different cultures throughout the world (Triandis & Lambert, 1980).

The goals of multicultural therapy and counseling are different from those of the traditional schools of personality change. The Multicultural

Model has two categories of goals: individual, and institutional, or societal goals.

The individual goals emphasize self-understanding and self-acceptance. The model also encourages understanding the effects of person environment fit on personality development and adjustment. Multicultural therapy seeks to empower the client to produce significant environmental changes.

Institutional and societal goals focus on the identification and elimination of barriers to multicultural development, and on replacing those barriers with positive politics of diversity in families, institutions, and in society as a whole.

Multicultural therapy and counseling works towards the creation of a truly multicultural society, striving to develop a world of peace, understanding, and cooperation in which each person's individuality is respected. In this model, the diversity of society is viewed as a potential teacher and catalyst to the total development of the personality.

In today's world, all people who live and work in diverse institutions and societies are prone to feeling marginal, confused, and perhaps even threatened from time to time. The demands for both cultural and cognitive flexibility in a pluralistic society can be felt in all facets of life. They are part of daily interactions in business, education, community services, religion, and government. The Multicultural Model of psychotherapy provides a useful set of coping techniques as well as a world view that is useful to everyone living and working in pluralistic environments.

Acknowledgments

I wish to express my gratitude to Terry Foster for her help in editing the manuscript and in suggesting many changes that were incorporated into the text. I am also grateful to Lilly Arvizu for her help in editing the final drafts of the manuscript and to Robin Sanford for typing the final draft. I owe a special debt of gratitude to the graduate students who have participated in my seminar on multicultural psychotherapy; their ideas and suggestions were invaluable and contributed immeasurably to the development of the Multicultural Model of Psychotherapy and Counseling.

Chapter 1

Feeling Different: One of the Major Mental Health Problems of Our Time

CASE STUDIES

Case Study 1: Imelda M.

Imelda is a 16-year old Hispanic high school student who attempted suicide by swallowing some two hundred aspirin tablets. She was despondent because of the break-up of a three-year relationship with her boyfriend. During an interview in the hospital she said, "I wanted to die because I am alone and I'm different. I've lost the only person who accepted me as I really am. I have always been different from my parents, from my teachers, and from most of the other students. My boyfriend was the only one who understood me. No one will accept me as I am. They are always trying to change me."

Case Study 2: Harold H.

Harold, a 35-year-old Anglo engineer and part-owner of a computer software company, came to the author in a distressed state. He explained, "I don't feel I'm as effective and capable as I used to be. I don't really belong anywhere—not with my family, not with my partners, not even with my own parents." During the initial psychotherapy session, he talked about how he had always tried to win his father's love and admiration.

> Dad always preferred my older brother; nothing I did changed that. I tried to show him that I could be successful in business because that is what I thought he wanted. And to be a success, I had to ignore my wife and kids. Well, I'm a success now, and this hasn't changed anything with my father.

1

Now I'm in danger of losing my family while my partners are complaining that I don't seem to have my heart in my work anymore. I honestly don't know what's happening. My entire world is falling apart, and I can't do anything about it. I just don't feel like I belong anywhere. I can't connect with anyone anymore. I'm so alone.

Case Study 3: Troy M.

Troy, an African-American middle school student, was taken by his parents to see the author because of his increasing alienation from his family and because of his preoccupation with a fantasy of being from another planet. During the initial interview Troy told the therapist:

> I don't fit in with the White kids in my enriched classes; the other Black kids in my school won't have anything to do with me. They say my parents are rich, and they avoid me because my mother is a teacher.
>
> At home my mother is always on me to make better grades. My father only cares about his garden and fishing. I don't belong at school or with my family. I must be from another world—I'm too different to be human.

Case Study 4: Wanda J.

Wanda, a 32-year-old Anglo college graduate and mid-level manager in a large corporation, sought counseling because she was depressed and worried about her drinking. She indicated that she is the only female manager in the office where she works. She said:

> I feel so different from the other people I work with. Drinking makes me feel comfortable with the other members of the management team, but I'm worried about my drinking—my father is an alcoholic.
>
> I'm also concerned that I'm changing so much in order to fit in with the men in my management team that my husband can't love me anymore because I'm not the woman he married. I drink at home to feel closer to him; the only time we make love is when we've both been drinking.

FEELING DIFFERENT

The four people described here have one thing in common: they are in crises because they feel different from those around them. The feeling of being different is accompanied by feelings of alienation and loneliness. People who feel different feel misunderstood.

This feeling of being different is typical among members of minority groups (for the purposes of this book, "minority group" is used to refer to any group that is in some way different from the societal ideal); but this feeling is also familiar to anyone who has felt pressured by society to conform.

The common dynamic in the "differentness syndrome" is mismatch. The victim of mismatch feels alienation from individuals, groups and cultures, and institutions that play an important part in his or her life. What are the causes of mismatch? The cultural and individual differences which make each of us unique are also responsible for making us feel mismatched to others and to our environments. The majority society imposes pressures on us to conform, to abandon our individuality, and to force ourselves into the fictional ideal molds and patterns created by those who have power and influence (Katz & Taylor, 1988). Since not many of us fit these patterns in every way, we are made to feel different and inferior, as if there were something wrong with us. The end result is that we reject our selves, or at least part of our true selves, in order to "fit in" and to appear less different.

The Mismatch Syndrome

The four clients described earlier in this chapter felt mismatched to the important people and institutions in their lives. They felt alone, hopeless, and misunderstood. They exhibited a number of common symptoms: self-rejection, depression, emphasis on the negative, rigidity of thinking and problem-solving, and attempts to escape reality. All of these symptoms are part of the mismatch syndrome. Let us examine the four cases in more detail to see how pressures to conform are related to the syndrome.

Imelda M. Imelda was reared in a traditional society, typical of rural communities in the U.S.-Mexico border region. Unusual to the traditional pattern, however, were her parents' divorce and her interest in sports; she was a member of the varsity basketball and volleyball teams.

Imelda felt mismatched to the important authority figures in her life— her father, stepmother, grandparents, and teachers. Her parents and grandparents pressured her to abandon her interest in sports because it was not consistent with their perception of how a proper young woman should behave.

Her teachers did not like Imelda's attempts to make classes more relevant to herself and to her fellow students. When she asked her teachers to relate what she was being taught to her own experiences, as well as to those of her classmates, her behavior was interpreted as rebellious and lacking in respect. Although Imelda's peers admired her feats on the basketball and volleyball courts, they saw her as an oddball, as not being feminine enough, and rarely included her in their social activities outside of school. Thus, Imelda was often lonely, isolated, and misunderstood. Only with her boyfriend did she feel comfortable and accepted. When he broke up with her, she felt her life had come to an end.

Harold H. Harold grew up in the suburban-modernistic world of the San Francisco Bay Area. His feelings of being different began when he started to compare himself to his older brother and when he tried to win his father's love and approval. His father and his brother were well matched to each other; they were both competitive and interested in electronics. Harold, on the other hand, was cooperative in orientation, and his interests were in art and music.

Pressures to conform increased for Harold after his brother's death. To please and comfort his father, he changed his academic interests. His own personality prevailed, however, with his choice of a wife, and with his attempts to establish a sense of community and leadership in his place of work. At home however, he became more like his father—distant and uninvolved with his children.

As he felt pressured by his wife and children to become more involved with them and more sensitive to their needs, Harold began to feel more uncomfortable about neglecting his partners. When Harold came to therapy he was confused, believing it was impossible to please all of the important people in his life. He also felt like a failure because despite making what he considered to be superhuman efforts to please his father, he had not succeeded, and the relationship with him was fraught with conflict and misunderstanding.

Troy C. Troy was reared in a traditional rural African-American and Anglo community. He was socialized in an African-American neighborhood during the first six years of his life, but when he began school, his family moved to a predominantly Anglo neighborhood. He was one of very few African-Americans in a predominantly Anglo school, and was the only African-American in his enriched classes.

Troy felt mismatched to both of his parents; his mother always demanded that he do better in school and he perceived her as being distant and cold. His father, though more personable and warmer, was primarily interested in fishing and gardening.

Troy felt alienated from his Anglo classmates. While he preferred to do things with others and was introspective, he perceived his Anglo classmates as competitive and analytical in their personality styles. They did not share his interest in literature and poetry. Troy's African-American peers did not accept him, feeling that he spent too much time with the Anglos, and labeling him and his family as "rich".

Troy retreated to a world of fantasy—he read a great deal of science fiction and, after seeing the movie *The Brother from Another Planet,* concluded that he was an alien.

Wanda C. Wanda grew up in an urban-modernistic city on the East Coast. Her feelings of being different originated from growing up in a dysfunctional family with an alcoholic father. As a child, Wanda had been reluctant to invite friends to visit her home because of her father's drinking. She adopted the role of "hero child," believing that she had to be perfect to ensure that her family would stay together.

Wanda grew up admiring families in traditional cultures, seeing them as warm, cooperative, and caring. Eventually she married a Hispanic man who came from a traditional family and who provided her with the stability she had been lacking in her own family. Unfortunately, when her career forced her into an impersonal and competitive style, her change in personality threatened her husband and children and the idyllic life she had developed with them.

Wanda felt strong pressures to conform both from her new job and her family. Confused and threatened, she felt as though she were trying to live in two separate worlds. Her mismatch syndrome was manifested in mismatch shock; no matter how much she tried to cope in either environment, she felt she was failing. Like her father, she began turning to alcohol for escape.

SUMMARY

The mismatch syndrome—feelings of differentness, of depression, of not belonging or being accepted—is common in societies that stress conformity to certain fictional ideals. Although women and members of minority groups have been the most frequent victims of this syndrome, in one way or another almost everyone has had this experience. How can therapists and counselors help the victims of conformity pressures? Developments in the psychology of differentness have introduced a new paradigm as well as models of personality and counseling (Comaz-Diaz & Griffith, 1988; Parker, 1988; Pedersen, 1988) based on the realities of adjustment to a pluralistic society. These new developments encourage multicultural development in an atmosphere of peace and cooperation.

Chapter 2

Emergence of a Psychology of Differentness and Pluralism: The Multicultural Person-Environment Fit Paradigm

The task facing the therapist who tries to help a victim of the mismatch syndrome is a challenging one. This task is all the more difficult because mainstream theories and techniques of counseling and psychotherapy ignore cultural and individual differences.

PSYCHOLOGY AND COLONIZATION

Although psychology began as the science of individual differences, it has, over the years, abandoned its original mission and has instead become the science of the mean and of the mode. For the most part, the uniqueness of people has been forgotten and the emphasis has been on what the people in power have felt is the most desirable composite of personality or adjustment, or on what was considered a standard of adjustment and health.

Because of the redefinition of its mission, psychology has been used by conformists and enculturationists to force those who are disenfranchised—the colonized, the recent immigrant, the poor—to become like the mythical ideal valued by those in power.

European Powers and Colonization

France, England, Portugal, and Spain had extensive colonization programs that made use of psychological theories, concepts, and techniques.

6

Detribalization, and the accompanying enculturation programs in particular, were essential to the European colonial powers. These colonization programs were reflections of the colonizers' belief that their culture and life style were superior to those of the colonized (Collins, 1954). The detribalization and enculturation efforts of the colonization programs were attempts to break up old loyalties and allegiances of the members of colonized populations to their families, tribes, religions, regional areas, and countries.

The principal objective of these efforts was to replace old loyalties with a total allegiance to the culture and religion of the colonizer. The enculturation program adopted by the British government was particularly thorough—it involved sending members of the native populations to England where they were taught English, were trained in Christianity, were instructed in British history, and were introduced to British culture. After several years, these people were returned to their home lands to assist the British in the implementation of enculturation programs. This emphasis on the use of psychology to ensure the success of colonization programs provided some of the early impetus for the development of cross-cultural psychology in Europe.

The colonization programs followed by European countries in general, and the application of psychological concepts to understanding the behavior of members of the colonized populations in particular, helped shape a world view of those peoples whose culture and life style differed from those of the colonizers. This world view has had a significant impact on the development of personality and clinical psychology as well as of psychiatry with respect to individual and cultural diversity.

The U.S.—From Inclusivist to Exclusivist Melting Pot

In the United States, there was an initial acceptance of individual and cultural differences. Conditions unique to the American continent produced changes in the class-bound institutions brought by English colonists. Institutions brought by immigrants from non-English homelands were similarly modified by the new environment.

The evolution of institutions which were uniquely American in an environment which was more accepting of cultural and individual diversity than Europe inspired the French writer Crevecoeur (1904) to posit a new social theory: America as a melting pot.

Crevecoeur conceived of the evolving American society not as a slightly modified England, but as a totally new cultural and biological blend. In the United States, the genetic strains and folkways of Europe mixed indiscriminately in the political pot of the emerging nation, were fused by the fires of American influence and interaction into a distinctly new American personality. This inclusivistic version of the melting pot was transformed into a more exclusivist version as more people from Eastern Europe, Asia, and Latin America began to immigrate into the United States. What finally emerged was a forced conformity model.

The major principles of this exclusivist melting pot are best described in the words of E. P. Cubberly, a leading American educator. Describing the new immigrants from Southern and Eastern Europe as illiterate, docile, and lacking in self reliance and initiative, he identified the goals of the American public education system for immigrant parents and their children:

> . . . everywhere these people settle in groups or settlements, and . . . set up their national manners, customs and observances. Our task is to break up these groups or settlements, to assimilate and amalgamate these people as part of our American race, and to implant in their children, as far as can be done, the Anglo-Saxon conception of righteousness, law and order and our popular government, and to awaken in them a reverence for our democratic institutions and for those things in our national life which we as a people hold to be of abiding worth. (1909, pp. 15–16)

Psychology as a Source of Tools for Enculturation and Conformism

Psychology became a prime source of tools for educators and for mental health professionals who forced conformity on "the different." One of the major tools borrowed from psychology by conformists and enculturationists (and still widely used today) is the intelligence test.

As Guthrie (1976) observed in his book *Even the Rat Was White,* tests of intellectual ability have been used by both psychologists and educators to try to prove that African-Americans and Mexican-Americans are intellectually inferior to Anglos, and that recent immigrants are of lower intelligence than mainstream Americans.

The first attempts to demonstrate that members of minority groups were intellectually inferior to Anglos were encouraged by Terman, the psychologist who revised the original scales for assessing intelligence developed by Alfred Binet in France. Terman stated that mental retardation "represents the level of intelligence which is very, very common among Spanish-Indians and Mexican families of the Southwest and also among Negroes. Their dullness appears to be racial" (1916, p.92). In addition, Terman went on to predict that when future intelligence testing of the aforementioned groups was undertaken, "there will be discovered enormously significant racial differences which cannot be wiped out by any scheme of mental culture."

The effort to use measures of intelligence to push enculturation conformity, as well as the ideas of cultural and racial superiority, also extended to the so-called "culture free" tests such as the Raven Progressive Matrices, (Raven, Court, & Raven, 1986). Cohen (1969) and Ramirez and Castaneda (1974) have observed that even these tests are biased in favor of field-independent cognitive styles and against the field-dependent or field-sensitive cognitive style that is characteristic of members of minority groups in the United States.

Another tool borrowed from psychology and used extensively for encouraging enculturation and conformism was the psychoanalytic theory of personality. Psychoanalytic theory was used extensively by European powers to justify their programs of colonization.

Mannoni (1960), a French psychoanalyst, published a paper on the psychology of colonization in which he concluded that colonization was made possible by an inherent need in subject populations to be dependent. He believed that this need for dependency was satisfied by the high degree of individualism and self-sufficiency characteristic of Europeans. In fact, Mannoni made it appear as though colonized populations were characterized by an unconscious desire for colonization: "Wherever Europeans have founded colonies of the type we are considering, it can be safely said that their coming was unconsciously expected—even desired—by the future subject peoples" (p. 644).

Psychoanalytic theory was also used to force conformity on women. The most widely used aspect of the theory was Freud's (1925) conceptualization of the sexual development of women that led him to conclude that women's superegos were not as highly developed as those of men, and that women suffered from "penis envy."

Still another tool borrowed from psychology by enculturationists and conformists were behavior modification techniques and approaches. Going hand in hand with the misuse of behavior modification with "the different" is the misclassification of children, adolescents, and adults of minority groups (Malgady, Rogler, & Constantino, 1987) who are incorrectly diagnosed as Attention Deficit Disorder, Conduct Disorder, Oppositional Defiant Disorder, or as Learning Disabled.

A person so categorized is subjected to "behavior shaping" or "behavior management" programs that attempt to change behavior and make it conform more closely to the mythical mode of the American middle class. These enculturation-conformity programs are being widely used in schools, prisons, mental hospitals, and in institutions for the mentally retarded or disabled.

In her book *Black Children: Their Roots, Culture, and Learning Styles,* Hale-Benson (1982) observes that:

> The emphasis of traditional education has been upon molding and shaping Black children so that they can fit into an educational process designed for Anglo-Saxon middle class children. We know that the system is not working because of the disproportionate number of Black children who are labeled hyperactive. (p. 1)

In a similar vein, Snowden and Todman (1982) postulated:

> In assessing assertiveness, some of the variety encountered will have cultural origins . . . those evaluating assertiveness are prone to standardize their conceptions of situations and behaviors, making unwarranted uniformity assumptions. As cultural differences are only dimly understood, they may be particularly easy to overlook. (p. 221)

ORIGINS OF THE PSYCHOLOGY OF DIFFERENTNESS

Despite the strong conformist and enculturation trends in the United States and Europe, strong voices of dissent began to make themselves heard as early as the late 1920s. A new psychology of differentness, of respect for individual and cultural differences, was being born.

Founders of the Psychology of Differentness

Horney. One of the earliest pioneers in the development of the psychology of differentness was Karen Horney, one of the first women psychoanalysts. Horney's story is truly a profile in courage (Quinn, 1987). She grew up in Germany, and although she was reared in a traditional Victorian family with a very authoritarian father, she succeeded in overcoming the conventions of her time by going to medical school and becoming an independent thinker.

She emigrated to the United States in the 1940s and worked with many female patients whose problems centered around oppression in a sexist society. Her own personal experiences, along with what she learned from her patients, led her to conclude that Freud's emphasis on penis envy in the dynamics of women's sexuality was inaccurate. She also discovered that the biological orientation of Freud's theory ignored important cultural realities: the powerless position of most women in society, and the central role of culture in personality dynamics.

Horney wrote:

> One can diagnose a broken leg without knowing the cultural background of the patient, but one would run a great risk in calling an Indian psychotic

because he told us that he had visions in which he believed. In the particular culture of these Indians the experience of visions and hallucinations is regarded as a special gift, a blessing from the spirits. (1937, p. 14–15)

Horney's views were not generally accepted during her lifetime, and the strong opposition to her views by members of the New York Psychoanalytic Society eventually led to her resignation from that body.

Sanchez. Another founder of the psychology of differentness was the Hispanic psychologist and educator George I. Sanchez. Sanchez was born and reared in northern New Mexico. He received his doctorate from the University of California at Berkeley.

Criticizing efforts by Anglo psychologists and educators to prove that Hispanic and African-American children were intellectually inferior to Anglo children, Sanchez (1932) made it clear that racial and ethnic superiority could not be claimed because a review of the literature on intellectual testing indicated that environmental and linguistic factors were significantly related to performance on intelligence tests.

Sanchez objected to those who would simply translate a test from English into Spanish and expect it to accurately assess the intelligence of bilingual children. He repeatedly pointed out that the validity of any test was limited to the normative sample on which it was based.

Sanchez also claimed that data on genetics and heredity were being garbled in order to champion the superiority of one group over others. He directed his attacks against those who blindly accepted the doctrine of genetic superiority while disregarding the importance of such fundamental factors as personal, social, economic, and environmental differences and their effects on intellectual assessment.

Sanchez's views were supported by the research findings of an African-American educator, Horace Mann Bond. In a classic article (1927), Bond selected African-American children from the homes of professionals and the middle class rather than from the laboring class, the favored source of subjects for Anglo psychologists. Using the Stanford Binet Test to test the children, he showed that 63 percent of the African-American children achieved scores above 106; 47 percent had intelligence scores equal to or exceeding 122; and 26 percent had scores over 130.

Bond concluded that these children "were not out of the ordinary . . . the same sort of group could be selected in any Negro community" provided that the sociocultural background of the subjects was similar to the one he tested (1927, p. 257).

Fanon. Another pioneer in the differentness movement in psychology was Franz Fanon, an African-Martiniquean psychiatrist. Fanon emphasized the importance of sociocultural realities and especially the influence of racism and oppression in the personality development of colonized peoples (Bul-han, 1985).

Fanon criticized the psychoanalytic theories of Freud, Jung, and Adler for their Eurocentric orientation. In his book *Black Skins: White Masks* (1967), he rejected Freud's ontogenetic perspective and Jung's phylogenetic specu-lations: "It will be seen that the black man's alienation is not an individual question. Beside phylogeny and ontogeny stands sociogeny." He also re-jected the notion of the Oedipus Complex and sought to explain personal-ity dynamics in terms of socio-historical and cultural realities. Fanon re-jected Freud's argument that neurosis was an inescapable consequence of all cultures. He instead saw neurosis as the expression of a given culture: "Even neurosis, every abnormal manifestation, every affective erethism . . . is the product of the cultural situation" (1967, p. 152).

NEW WORLD VIEW OF MENTAL HEALTH AND PSYCHOLOGICAL ADJUSTMENT

In the 1960s and 1970s, new developments in psychology began to reflect the ideas of Horney, Fanon, and Sanchez. One of these movements was the development of Community Psychology as a legitimate area of study within psychology. Community Psychology was a true "psychology of the Americas" (Ramirez, 1983); that is, it reflected the unique ideology emerging from the experiences specific to peoples of the Americas. This ideology was reflected in the melting pot philosophy in the United States and that of the Mestizo (the cultural and genetic mixture of Native-Ameri-cans and Europeans) in Mexico and other regions of Latin America.

Specifically, Community Psychology had its roots in the community mental health movement, and in applied sociology. One of the major contributions of Community Psychology to the psychology of different-ness was what Julian Rappaport (1977) referred to as the paradigm of person-environment fit: respect for human diversity, the right to be dif-ferent, and the belief that human problems are those of person-environ-ment fit, rather than of incompetent or inferior people, or inferior psycho-logical or cultural environments.

The major impact of this new paradigm on psychology was most felt in Latin America (Marin, 1975), where psychologists began to turn to their own cultures and to the experiences of their own countries and peoples to develop new approaches to psychological research and intervention, as well as new conceptual frameworks for interpreting the data they col-lected.

The earliest developments in the psychology of differentness came in the areas of women's psychology in Europe, and of African-American and Hispanic psychology in the United States. The Civil Rights Movement of the 1960s provided the impetus for the development of ethnic psychologies as well as a psychology of women based on the writings of Karen Horney, Franz Fanon, and George Sanchez. These perspectives were true psychologies of the Americas.

These new approaches disclaimed the emphasis on universals in psychology, and instead emphasized the importance both of sociocultural environments and of the effects of minority status and oppression on personality development and functioning. They emphasized values as reflected in socialization practices and how these values affected personality development. In addition, there was an emphasis on how oppression and minority status were related to the development of pathology and problems of identity. In the case of women, the emphasis was on development of self-in-relation—that is, the conflict between attachment and separation because of the way in which women are socialized, and because of expectations placed on them by society.

These new movements in psychology led to a new paradigm that now guides the work of the psychology of differentness—the Multicultural Person-Environment Fit Paradigm. This paradigm represents an extension and amplification of the person-environment paradigm because of its assumption that it is important to synthesize and amalgamate diversity in order to arrive at multicultural identities and perspectives on life, and new approaches to solutions of problems. These new outlooks can lead to understanding among different peoples and groups—the basis of peace and cooperation.

CHARACTERISTICS OF THE MULTICULTURAL PERSON-ENVIRONMENT FIT WORLD VIEW

The Multicultural Person-Environment Fit World View is based on a number of assumptions:

1. There are no inferior people, cultures, or groups in terms of gender, ethnicity, race, economics, religion, region, or language.
2. Problems of maladjustment are not the result of inferior peoples or groups, but rather of mismatch between people, or between people and their environments.
3. Every individual, group, or culture has positive contributions to make to personality development and to a healthy adjustment to life.
4. People who are willing to learn from others, and from groups and

cultures different from their own, acquire multicultural building blocks (coping techniques and perspectives) which are the basis of multicultural personality development and multicultural identity.

5. The synthesis and amalgamation of personality building blocks acquired from different peoples, groups, and cultures occurs when the person with multicultural potential works toward the goals of understanding and cooperation among diverse groups and peoples in a pluralistic society.

6. The synthesis and amalgamation of personality building blocks from diverse origins results in the development of a multicultural personality and a multicultural identity—the ultimate in personality development and psychological adjustment in a pluralistic society.

SUMMARY

The struggle against the idea that some cultures, groups, or people are superior to others has led to the development of the Multicultural Person-Environment Fit World View. In recent years a model of psychotherapy and counseling based on this new paradigm has begun to evolve. This new model not only helps the victims of mismatch, but also empowers them to help create a better world—a world in which individual and cultural differences will be respected and in which pluralism will be viewed as a resource for the development of mutual understanding, cooperation, and self-actualization.

Chapter 3
The Cognitive and Cultural Flex Theory of Personality

In her book *Neurosis and Human Growth* (1950), the psychoanalyst and pioneer feminist psychologist Karen Horney introduced the idea that a person becomes neurotic because of his or her attempts to live up to the "tyranny of the shoulds." That is, the neurotic person develops a self-image based on what others would like him or her to be, an idealized image, instead of developing a "true self."

The person becomes neurotic, developing a false self based on the "shoulds" of parents and important others. This false self is an idealized image which forces the person to conform to certain imposed idealized standards and results in the disavowal and suppression of the true self.

The "different" in society are most vulnerable to the "tyranny of the shoulds" because it is they who are most often targets of conformity and assimilation pressures. The autobiography of Richard Rodriguez (1983), *Hunger of Memory*, is a good example of how the "tyranny of the shoulds" works. Rodriguez tells a story of when he was in elementary school in Sacramento, California. The primary language of his family was Spanish, and he struggled in school because he did not know English well.

One day his teachers visited his parents and implied that if they wanted Richard to succeed in school, they would have to start speaking English at home. Convinced of this, his parents began speaking to Richard only in English. However, they continued to communicate with each other in Spanish. The change resulted in academic success for Richard, but the price paid was his psychological disorientation and emotional alienation from his family. He states that, "once I spoke English with ease, I came to feel guilty. I felt that I had shattered the intimate bond that once held the family close" (p. 30).

15

SCHOOLS AND CONFORMITY

For the "different," the strongest agents of conformity in society are often the schools. In their book *Cultural Democracy, Bicognitive Development and Education,* Ramirez and Castaneda (1974) argued that schools force conformity on children of minority groups through their assimilationist philosophies and predominant orientation; an Anglo, middle class teaching style and curriculum content. The message of the schools to minority children is very like that given to Richard Rodriguez: "If you want to succeed, you must reject your true self and be like us."

The pressures to assimilate and to conform are not restricted to members of minority groups. Anyone whose personality, life style, gender, value system, or physical characteristics makes him or her different from the majority, becomes the target of assimilation and conformity pressures of society—the "tyranny of the shoulds."

CULTURES, COMMUNITIES, FAMILIES, AND THE UNIQUE SELF

In *Cultural Democracy, Bicognitive Development and Education,* Ramirez and Castaneda (1974) point out that people have unique intellectual strengths, abilities, and skills. Additionally, people develop learning and problem-solving styles which reflect the values and belief systems of the culture, community, and family in which they were reared.

For example, Stodolsky and Lesser (1967) compared children of different ethnic groups on intellectual skills, finding that Chinese-American children did better at problems involving spatial skills. Jewish-American children, on the other hand, did better at tasks and problems requiring verbal ability.

Ramirez and Castaneda (1974), proposed that in order to ensure respect for the intellectual strengths and styles of learning of all children, schools need to adopt a philosophy of cultural democracy as well as teaching styles and approaches that match individual and cultural differences in learning styles.

The authors defined cultural democracy and teaching/learning and cultural styles match as follows:

1. *Educational philosophy of cultural democracy.* The opposite of assimilation, cultural democracy encourages schools to respect cultural, community, family, and individual differences in values and life styles. Values influence the socialization and teaching styles which in turn affect the development of certain learning and problem-solving styles. Figure 3.1 summarizes the relationships between sociocultural systems and individual differences in intellectual styles.

Values and belief systems of cultures, communities, families	$\longrightarrow$	Socialization patterns and teaching styles	$\longrightarrow$	Individual differences in problem solving and intellectual styles

FIGURE 3.1. Relationship Between Values and Personality

2. *Teaching and cultural styles match.* Teaching styles and styles of curriculum and testing are tailored to match the cultural styles of the students. Students and teachers are encouraged to develop multicultural orientations to life in a pluralistic learning environment.

3. *Teaching and learning styles match.* Teaching styles and styles of curriculum and testing are tailored to match the individual learning and problem-solving styles of the students. To achieve this, individual students and school personnel are encouraged to become flexible in their intellectual styles by learning unfamiliar teaching and learning styles in a supportive and accepting educational environment.

THE LINK BETWEEN CULTURAL AND COGNITIVE STYLES

Cultural Styles

Ramirez and Castaneda (1974) proposed that cultures, communities, and families can be classified on a traditionalism-modernism dimension with respect to their cultural styles. Modern life styles and belief systems encourage separation from family and community early in life. Modern orientations to socialization emphasize individual competition, and science is given great importance in explaining the mysteries of life.

Traditional life styles on the other hand, emphasize close ties to family and community throughout life. Traditional orientations emphasize cooperation and give spiritualism a greater importance in explaining life events.

There are several domains within the traditionalism-modernism dimension:

1. *Gender role definition:* Traditional environments tend to emphasize strict distinctions between gender roles, whereas modern environments encourage more flexible boundaries between these roles.

2. *Family identity:* Traditional environments foster strong family identities; modern environments emphasize individual identities.

3. *Sense of community:* Traditional cultural styles encourage a strong sense of community while modern environments emphasize individualism.

4. *Family identification:* Family loyalty and identification are emphasized in traditional communities while individual identities are more valued in modern societies.

5. *Time orientation:* People reared in traditional communities have a

stronger past and present time orientation while people who are more modernistic are oriented towards the future.

6. *Age status:* Traditional societies associate increasing age with increasing wisdom, whereas modern societies value the vitality of youth.

7. *Importance of tradition:* Traditional environments value traditional ceremonies as a reinforcement of history, whereas modern value orientations tend to view tradition as a potential barrier to progress.

8. *Subservience to convention and authority:* In traditional societies people are socialized to follow norms and conventions and to respect authority; in modern societies people are encouraged to question authority.

9. *Spirituality and religion:* Traditional societies emphasize the importance of spirituality and religion in life events; modern societies are characterized by an emphasis on science and secularism.

It was discovered that while rural environments are most commonly associated with traditional cultural orientations, and urban life styles usually reflect modernistic orientations to life (Panday & Panday, 1985; also Tharakan, 1987), research (Ramirez, 1987) has also shown that some people who live in urban environments tend to adhere to traditional values and, similarly, that there are residents of rural areas who tend to be modernistic in their cultural styles.

Cognitive Styles

The hypothesized relationships between values and cognitive styles is summarized in Figure 3.2.

Ramirez, Castaneda, and their colleagues identified the following learning behaviors as characteristic of children who tended to be field sensitive or field independent. These are clustered into four categories shown in Table 3.1.

Additional research on the relationship of sociocultural environments to intellectual styles in children and college students (Ramirez, 1983) led Ramirez and his colleagues to expand the theory of learning styles "flex" (the ability to switch styles to conform to environmental demands) to include other characteristics of personality. They posited that a person's unique self is made up of much more than just learning and intellectual

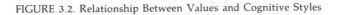

| Modern cultures, communities and families | → | Modern teaching and socialization styles | → | Field independent learning styles |
| Traditional cultures, communities and families | → | Traditional teaching and socialization styles | → | Field sensitive learning styles |

FIGURE 3.2. Relationship Between Values and Cognitive Styles

Table 3.1 Characteristics of Field Sensitive and Field Independent Children

Domain	Field Sensitive	Field Independent
Relationship to Peers	1. Likes to work with others to achieve common goals.	1. Prefers to work independently.
	2. Likes to assist others.	2. Likes to compete and gain individual recognition.
	3. Is sensitive to feelings and opinions of others.	3. Task-oriented; is inattentive to social environment when working.
Relationship to Teacher	1. Openly expresses positive feelings for teacher.	1. Avoids physical contact with teacher.
	2. Asks questions about teacher's taste and personal experiences; seeks to become like teacher.	2. Formal interactions with teacher; restricted to tasks at hand.
Instructional Relationship to Teacher	1. Seeks guidance and demonstration from teacher.	1. Likes to try new tasks without teacher's help.
	2. Seeks rewards which strengthen relationship with teacher.	2. Impatient to begin tasks; likes to finish first.
	3. Is highly motivated by working individually with teacher.	3. Seeks nonsocial rewards.
Thinking Style	1. Functions well when objectives are carefully explained or modeled	1. Focuses on details and parts of things.
	2. Deals well with concepts in humanized or story format.	2. Deals well with math and science concepts.
	3. Functions well when curriculum content is relevant to personal interests and experiences.	3. Likes discovery or trial-and-error learning.

styles. They were able to show that field independent and field sensitive styles are also reflected in the ways in which people communicate and relate to others, in the rewards that motivate them, and in the manner in which they teach, parent, supervise, and counsel others. The behaviors which differentiated field sensitive from field independent personality styles are listed in Table 3.2.

Table 3.2. Personality Characteristics of Field Sensitive and Field Independent People

Domain	Field Sensitive	Field Independent
Communications	1. Tends to personalize communications by referring to own life experiences, interests and feelings.	1. Tends to be impersonal and to–the–point in communications.
	2. Tends to focus more on non-verbal than on verbal communication.	2. Tends to focus more on verbal than on non-verbal communication.
Interpersonal Relationships	1. Open and outgoing in social settings.	1. Reserved and cautious in social settings.
	2. Presents as warm and informal.	2. Presents as distant and formal.
Motivation	1. Values social rewards which strengthen relationships with important others.	1. Seeks non-social rewards.
	2. Motivation is related to achievement for others (family, team, ethnic/racial group, etc.).	2. Motivation is related to self-advancement.
Teaching, Parenting, Supervisory, and Counseling Relationships	1. Focuses on relationship with student, child, supervisee, or client.	1. Focuses on task or goal.
	2. Is informal and self-disclosing.	2. Is formal and private.

Ramirez, Castaneda, and their colleagues (Ramirez, 1983) discovered that the personalities of most individuals are a unique combination of field independent and field sensitive elements. Nevertheless, each person seems to have a definite preference for one style or the other. Style preference at any given time was often dependent on the type of demands made by the setting or task. For example, a person might be preferred field sensitive in a learning or problem-solving situation, but be preferred field independent in a social setting. Research (Ramirez, 1983) on successful children and college students, however, revealed that they tended to be more flexible in their styles as compared to their less successful peers. It was also discovered that the more successful students were flexible in both cultural and cognitive domains. That is, these children, adolescents, and young adults could shuttle between the different cognitive and cultural styles.

Life history and family and community research (Ramirez, Cox, & Castaneda, 1977; Ramirez, 1987) with students having different degrees of flex showed that those subjects who were the most flexible had been influenced by cultures, communities, and families whose life styles and institutions represented a mixture of traditional and modern values (see Figure 3.2). It was also discovered that in certain families, evidence of the ability to flex can be found in members of different generations (Buriel, 1981). A strong possibility exists, then, that propensity for flex is inherited.

PERSONALITY FLEX

Research focusing on personality flex led to the identification of its three components: (a) the degree of development of the major cognitive (field sensitive or field independent) and cultural (traditional or modern) styles; (b) the ability to shuttle between the major styles within the cognitive and cultural domains; and (c) the ability to combine these major cognitive and cultural styles to develop a multicultural cognitive style (combination of field independent and field sensitive) and cultural style (combination of traditional and modern). All three characteristics of flex were found to be important in determining coping effectiveness: People who were found to be well developed in only one of the two cognitive and cultural styles were not as effective in coping as those who were able to shuttle between the two styles, or to combine the major cultural and cognitive styles to arrive at new multicultural combinations.

COGNITIVE FLEX

Ramirez and Castaneda identified three components of cognitive flex or bicognition: (a) the maximum development of all domains of field sensitive and field independent cognitive styles; (b) the ability to shuttle between the field sensitive and field independent styles to meet different environmental demands; and (c) the ability to combine elements of both field sensitive and field independent styles to develop new multicultural cognitive styles.

To assess the degree of cognitive flex, Ramirez and Castaneda and their colleagues (Ramirez et al. 1978) developed observation instruments and personality inventories that assessed bicognition. These instruments, briefly described below, are presented in their entirety in chapter 8.

The cognitive styles Behavioral Observation Instrument is an observational rating scale that lists field independent and field sensitive behaviors in five domains:

- communications
- interpersonal relationships

- motivation
- teaching, parenting, supervising, and counseling
- learning and problem solving.

Cognitive flex is defined by both degree and type. Degree can be assessed by examining behavioral ratings that indicate how developed a person is in both of the styles—the degree of balance within the five domains listed above. Type of flex is determined in two ways: (a) the extent to which a person can combine behaviors which are characteristic of each of the styles to develop multicultural coping techniques (a composite of elements of both styles) and (b) the extent to which a person can use field sensitive and field independent behaviors in different domains (e.g., the person is competitive in a setting in which individual competition is emphasized, such as testing, and is cooperative in situations which require working with others to achieve a common goal).

The Bicognitive Orientation to Life Scale (BOLS) is a personality inventory composed of items which reflect the degree of preference for field sensitive or field independent cognitive styles in different life domains. Cognitive flex is assessed by determining the degree of agreement (from Strongly Disagree to Strongly Agree) with items that reflect preference for either field independent or field sensitive cognitive styles.

For example:

1. I have always done well in math and science courses. (field independent)
2. I have always done well in social science and history courses. (field sensitive)

Flex is also determined by arriving at a balance score obtained by adding points (Agree $= 1$, Strongly Agree $= 2$, Disagree $= -1$, and Strongly Disagree $= -2$), and examining the difference between total field independent and field sensitive scores.

The type of flex is assessed by examining the life domains (family, education, world of work, etc.) in which agreement between field independent and field sensitive items is equally strong. The extent to which field sensitive and field independent characteristics are combined to develop new styles of coping cannot be assessed with the BOLS.

CULTURAL FLEX

Ramirez and Castaneda (1974) identified four components of cultural flexibility:

- subscribing to values and belief systems which are representative of both traditional and modern cultures, groups, and families;

- being able to shuttle between traditional and modern groups and situations or activities;
- being able to combine traditional and modern values and belief systems in order to evolve new multicultural styles; and
- feeling identified with both traditional and modern families, cultures, and institutions.

Three approaches (Ramirez, 1983) have been developed to assess cultural flex: the Traditionalism-Modernism Inventory, the Multicultural Experience Inventory, and a Life History Interview Schedule.

The Traditionalism-Modernism Inventory is a personality inventory developed by Ramirez and Doell (1982) that assesses the degree of identification with traditional and modern values and belief systems. The instrument yields scores indicating the degree of agreement with items reflecting traditionalism or modernism as with the BOLS described above. The degree of flex can be determined by examining the difference between the total traditionalism and total modernism scores as well as by looking at the degree of agreement with the traditional and modern items in the different domains of life (family, gender roles, time orientation, etc.). Type of flex can be assessed by examining the degree of flex within each domain. For example, a person whose personality is characterized by cultural flex in the child socialization domain, expresses agreement with both of the items below:

1. Children should be taught to be loyal to their families. (traditional)
2. Children should be taught to be independent of their families at an early age. (modern)

The Life History Schedule focuses on development and expressions of cultural flex in the different periods of life, as well as on the extent of actual participation in both traditional and modern families, cultures, groups, and institutions. In addition, the life history also identifies the type of cultural flex by examining the degree to which a person has been able to combine modern and traditional values and belief systems to arrive at multicultural values and world views.

The Multicultural Experience Inventory (Ramirez, 1983) is a questionnaire that focuses on personal history and behavior in three areas: (a) demographic and linguistic; (b) socialization history; and (c) degree of multicultural participation in the past as well as in the present. The degree of cultural flex is determined by the extent to which a person has been exposed to certain languages and value systems, and the degree to which the person has participated in, and is actively participating in and interacting with peoples of different cultures and groups in his or her social environment.

A COGNITIVE AND CULTURAL
FLEX THEORY OF PERSONALITY

Life history research (Ramirez et al., 1978) with people who scored high in both the cultural and cognitive flex domains led to the finding that socialization and life experiences were related to the development of personality flex.

Socialization and life experiences are two subcomponents of life history. Information on socialization history obtained from life histories of people who scored high in cognitive and cultural flex, showed that as compared with those with low scores, they had had parents and other socialization agents (teachers, employers, coaches, peers, and neighbors) whose attitudes toward diversity had been positive.

Not only did their socialization agents tend to hold positive attitudes towards diversity, the origins of those with high scores also reflected diversity: they were members of different ethnic, racial, religious, regional, and socioeconomic groups. In terms of the life experiences component of their personal history, what seemed to be most important was the degree of exposure to diversity challenges — that is, situations in which the person had to learn a new language, or a new way of relating to others, or a new way of solving a problem because the language, relationship style, or problem solving approach to which they were accustomed was not effective in a new setting (Ramirez, 1983).

The people who were most flexible were those who had lived in many different cultures, communities, or regions and who had attended schools with a diverse composition of student body and staff. In addition, the number and type of positive or negative experiences with diversity seemed to play an important role in the development of flexibility. For example, a person who had always been accepted by others different from him or herself tended to show more flex development than a person who had been rejected or discriminated against.

History also appeared to have a direct relationship to the second major component in flex development — motivation. Life history data (Ramirez et al., 1977) showed that both the degree of attraction to diversity and the degree of openness of the person's learning-experience filter, were critical subcomponents of motivation. That is, people who were the most flexible also seemed to be those who were most attracted to diversity, as well as those most willing to learn from diversity when they were exposed to it.

Motivation appeared to be reflected in a person's degree of willingness to take risks in diversity challenges. The person whose early history had provided him or her with positive attitudes toward diversity and with a basic foundation for multicultural development, was also the one most likely to seek diversity challenges and to benefit from these experiences.

The third major component in the development of flexibility concerned the nature of the pool of resources available for personality development and for coping with the demands of life. This reservoir of resources could vary both in size and in degree of heterogeneity and diversity—the ethnic, racial, religious, age-related, regional, and socioeconomic mix. The more experience individuals had had with different peoples, cultures, groups, communities, and families, and the greater the variety of diversity challenges they had taken, the greater the size and heterogeneity of their personality resource pool.

The fourth major component of the flex theory of personality concerned multicultural patterns of behavior. That is, once a person had a heterogenous mix of personality resources in his or her repertoire, he or she was able to behave like a multicultural person—to flex culturally and cognitively (Garza, et al., 1982). In the early phases of development, personality building elements and resources in the individual's repertoire are exclusively linked to the cultural, socioeconomic, sexual, racial, religious, political, and geographic contexts in which they were learned. Therefore, adaptation to new cultural environments and situations is an important precursor to the development of multicultural life styles and identities.

This sort of challenge encourages the individual to reorganize and synthesize the resources and elements in his or her repertoire so that efforts to adapt involve the formation of combinations of resources and elements learned from different cultures, environments, and peoples. The resultant coping techniques and orientations to life are pluralistic. For example, in order to achieve consensus in a group whose members are diverse, the leader must arrive at a pluralistic leadership style and a pluralistic perspective on problems which are representative of the diversity which exists in that group (Garza, et al., 1982).

The fifth and final component of the flex theory is the development of multicultural identities. Being exposed to diversity and challenges for multicultural adaptation, a person continuously modifies both his or her self-picture and philosophy of life. Eventually, the person makes a definite commitment to growth by continuing to seek such challenges (Adler, 1974; Ramirez, 1983).

It is at this point that people begin to develop a multicultural identity. That is, they no longer see themselves as products of any one particular culture or group, but, instead, express a strong, life-long commitment to the well-being of all peoples, cultures, and groups (Ramirez, 1983). Figure 3.3 summarizes this process.

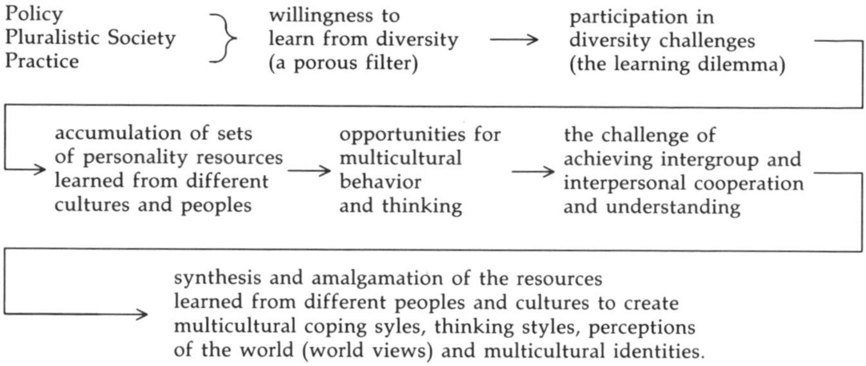

Policy   ⎫   willingness to   participation in
Pluralistic Society ⎬   learn from diversity ⟶   diversity challenges
Practice   ⎭   (a porous filter)   (the learning dilemma)

       accumulation of sets   opportunities for   the challenge of
⟶   of personality resources ⟶ multicultural   ⟶ achieving intergroup and
       learned from different   behavior   interpersonal cooperation
       cultures and peoples   and thinking   and understanding

       synthesis and amalgamation of the resources
⟶   learned from different peoples and cultures to create
       multicultural coping syles, thinking styles, perceptions
       of the world (world views) and multicultural identities.

FIGURE 3.3. Model of Multicultural Personality Development

SUMMARY

The critical concepts of the cultural and cognitive flex theory of personality are traditional and modern cultural styles, and field sensitive, field independent, and bicognitive styles of cognition. These concepts are useful in understanding multicultural personality development and fuctioning.

Chapter 4

Cultural and Cognitive Match and Mismatch in Psychological Adjustment

The flex theory of personality attempts to explain problems of maladjustment as degrees of match and mismatch between individuals and their environments. Match and mismatch are assessed in two domains: cognitive and cultural.

Both of these domains have several subdomains, or areas. It is possible for a person to be well matched in certain subdomains while being mismatched in others. A person can, for example, be well matched to peers in communication and interpersonal relationship styles but at the same time be mismatched in learning and problem-solving styles.

In order to demonstrate how the flex theory of personality can be used to assess the degree of psychological adjustment in terms of degrees of match and mismatch in the cognitive and cultural domains of a person's life, the theory will be applied to the four cases introduced in chapter 1.

CASE HISTORIES

The specific focus of this chapter is on trying to understand how problems of adjustment developed for Imelda, Harold, Troy, and Wanda from the perspective of cognitive and cultural mismatch. The information presented below was obtained from life history interviews done with each client. (The life history approach is discussed in detail in chapter 7.)

Although the principal focus of this book is on cultural and cognitive factors in maladjustment, general clinical considerations for each case are included to show that these were also of vital importance in the assessment of the clients.

Imelda M.

Background. Imelda was born and reared in a rural community located in the United States-Mexico border region of Texas. She was an only child. Her father, an accountant, and her mother, a homemaker, divorced when she was two years old. Following the divorce, Imelda's mother moved to a city in the northern part of Texas while Imelda and her father moved in with his parents.

When Imelda was twelve years old, her father remarried and the three of them moved to a house located next door to Imelda's grandparents. Imelda was shuttled between the two residences. Two years later, when Imelda was fourteen, Claudia, Imelda's half-sister was born.

As the half sister grew, Imelda began having conflicts with her stepmother. Imelda claimed that Claudia was spoiled and that she would often do things to aggravate her. Whenever she called the child's transgressions to the attention of her stepmother, she and Imelda would begin to argue. Imelda's perception was that her father would usually side with his wife against her. Gradually, Imelda became increasingly alienated from her parents and started to spend more and more time at her grandparents' home.

Imelda's grades plunged after her father remarried. Her teachers reported that she often acted out in class. Her only solace was sports and her relationship with Robert, her boyfriend. Her interest in sports, however, caused conflicts with her grandparents and most of her peers, who felt that her activities were not proper for a girl.

Her relationship with her boyfriend had started when she was fifteen, shortly after her father remarried. Her boyfriend's parents did not approve of the relationship because of Imelda's interest in sports and because she came from a broken home.

Imelda and Robert got along well because they were both alienated from their teachers and their parents. However, after much pressure from his parents, Robert succumbed to their wishes and reluctantly broke off the relationship with Imelda. This precipitated Imelda's attempt on her life.

Socialization and Life Experiences. Imelda was socialized in a very traditional Mexican-American community. After the divorce of her parents, she was socialized primarily by her grandparents, who strongly identified with traditional Hispanic culture. This culture encourages separation of gender roles and strict obedience to parents and other authority figures. In this type of cultural and familial setting, female children are encouraged to develop a preferred field sensitive cognitive style.

Because of his job as an accountant, a profession which requires analytical thinking and great attention to detail, it is probable that Imelda's father's preferred cognitive style was field independent, or bicognitive with a preference for field independence. In the elementary grades, Imelda's teachers had used field sensitive teaching styles and had encouraged cooperation and a sense of community. When she began junior high school, however, there was a decided shift in teaching style towards field independence, particularly in the enriched courses in which Imelda was enrolled. This style had a pronounced emphasis on individual competition and on analytical thinking.

Pattern of Adjustment. Imelda's relationships with her father, stepmother, and teachers were fraught with conflict. Her relationship with her natural mother seemed to be better than that with her father and stepmother, but the two rarely visited or telephoned each other. As Imelda became more involved in sports, her relationship with her grandparents began to deteriorate. Her only supportive relationship was with Robert, who, like Imelda, seemed to be preferred field sensitive in cognitive style. Robert was also supportive of Imelda's interest in sports. "Everyone seems to be against me except Robert. They're always criticizing me and trying to force me to live like they do. Why don't they accept me as I am instead of trying to change me?"

Symptoms. Imelda exhibited alienation from parents, teachers, and grandparents. She invested most of her time and energy in her relationship with her boyfriend at the expense of peer relationships with other students.

Analysis of Cognitive Style Mismatch

Imelda's preferred field sensitive style clashed with the preferred field independent style of her father and of her teachers.

Her grandparents were more field sensitive and less bicognitive than Imelda was.

Analysis of Cultural Mismatch

Imelda was modernistic in terms of gender roles as related to sports and in terms of challenging the authority of teachers. She was traditional with respect to cultural loyalty and religion.

Imelda's parents and grandparents, and Robert's parents were traditional with respect to gender roles.

General Clinical Considerations. Imelda should be evaluated for antidepressant medication. It should also be considered that her suicide attempt places her at risk for future suicidal behavior.

Harold H.

Background. Harold was born and reared in an upper middle class suburban community in the San Francisco Bay Area. Frank, a brother two years older than Harold died when Harold was sixteen. Harold's father was an engineer and an executive with a major computer electronics firm in the Silicon Valley. Harold's mother was an elementary school teacher.

Throughout childhood and early adolescence, Harold developed strong interests in art and music. He was closest to his mother during these years, and she encouraged his interests, providing solace for the constant frustration Harold felt because his father seemed to prefer his older brother to him.

Harold's father and Frank both had strong interests in sports, in fishing, in building airplane models, and in working with audio and television equipment. Harold had done his best to impress his father with his achievements in photography, painting, and music, but his father did not seem to appreciate this.

When Frank died in an automobile accident, Harold renewed his efforts to win his father's love and approval by trying to fill the gap which Frank had left—he abandoned his old interests, becoming more involved in sports and working harder at doing well in math and science. Harold's shift in interests did bring him closer to his father, but he never succeeded in developing the close relationship he longed for. To compensate for this, he vowed to prove to his father that he could be successful in business, something which his father had always wanted for Frank.

When Harold went to college he majored in engineering and computer science. When he was at the university he met Jan, whom he later married. Jan had been reared in a midsized Southern city. Her large family had close ties. Jan's major in college was art history. Through her, Harold could maintain a vicarious interest in art and music.

It was also while in college that Harold met the two friends who would become his partners. The three of them worked for four years with the same computer and electronics firm as Harold's father before they decided to establish a software company of their own.

Since the start-up of the new company was so demanding of Harold's time and energy, he made an informal contract with Jan: If Jan would agree to give up her career temporarily and do most of the parenting of their two children, Harold would assume most of the family responsibility once the company was on solid footing. Jan could then return to her career with Harold's full support. When Harold sought therapy, four years had passed since he had made his pact with Jan, and by then the company was successful, with two branch offices in Southern California.

Socialization and Life Experiences. Harold was socialized in a modernistic community, but in his home both traditional and modern values were represented. Harold's father was traditional in terms of rigidly defined gender roles, yet Harold's mother had a career, albeit one which was gender appropriate in terms of traditional cultural values.

Harold's father had a preferred field independent cognitive style, as reflected by his interests in electronics and engineering. His mother, a music major in college, and an elementary school music and art teacher, had a preferred field sensitive cognitive style. Thus, Harold was exposed to both cognitive styles and to both major cultural value systems.

His early interests in art and music attested to his preference for field sensitivity. It was not until his brother's death that he turned to field independent pursuits. His preference for field sensitivity and traditional values were again manifested in choosing Jan for his wife. It was also fortunate for Harold that he could express and develop some of his interests in field sensitive areas in his work through the development of computer graphics programs and through his leadership with the midlevel managers and workers.

Pattern of Adjustment. Harold's relationship with his father had remained strained. Harold felt that his many efforts to win his father's love and admiration had ended in failure. A major rupture developed in their relationship at the time Harold and his partners established their company. Harold thought his father would lend him money for the company and was devastated when, at the last minute, his father changed his mind. This caused a major rift between them. While Harold maintained contact with his mother, he cut off all communication with his father.

Over the years, Harold and Jan lost the intimacy they had enjoyed in the early years of their marriage. The long hours and many weekends that Harold devoted to the company, as well as the extensive traveling he had to do as part of his work, led him to feel that he was an outsider at home. As Harold said, "It got to the point that I had nothing to say to Jan or to the kids. When I came home from work I would just fix a drink and sit in front of the TV until it was time for supper. After supper I would return to work and come in after they had all gone to bed."

He rarely did anything with his children. At the time he came to therapy, Jan told him that if the situation did not change soon, and that if he did not live up to his side of the agreement, she would divorce him. With this shock Harold came to the realization that his behavior with his own children and wife was not unlike that of his father toward him and his mother—he was acting indifferent towards them.

Harold's business partners, on the other hand, were becoming unhappy with Harold's interest in moving the company in the direction of computer graphics. They were also noticing signs of "burn-out" in Harold—the charisma and leadership so important to employee loyalty and morale were disappearing as Harold retreated more and more into a world of his own.

Symptoms. Harold felt lonely, disoriented, and misunderstood. He was shocked by the ultimatum from his wife and by the realization that he had been behaving towards his children in the same way his father had behaved towards him. Harold was concerned with the fact that he had lost interest in technical software programs, the mainstay of the company's business over the years. He did not understand why the only thing which seemed to excite him at the present time was developments in computer graphics.

He was also concerned because he was feeling more and more alienated from his partners, who were not supportive of his interests. As a result, it was difficult for him to be enthusiastic about the future of the company. Thus, Harold was not investing as much time as in the past in maintaining the sense of community he had developed with midlevel managers, supervisors, and workers. As he said in his first therapy session, "My world is falling apart, and I don't know where to go from here."

Analysis of Cognitive Styles Mismatch

Harold's preferred cognitive style had been field sensitive in childhood and early adolescence, as demonstrated by his interests in art and music. In late adolescence and early adulthood, he had rejected this style and switched to the field independent style (computer science and engineering) to please his father and to fill the void left by Frank's death. At home with his wife and children, Harold was behaving as though he was preferred field independent, modeling his father's behavior. At work he had made use of his suppressed field sensitive style to provide leadership and a sense of community in maintaining a high level of employee satisfaction in

Harold's father's preferred field independent cognitive style, particularly in the interpersonal domain, mismatched Harold's, although Harold did try to match his father in the areas of work and career.

Jan's preferred style was probably field sensitive, and, in recent years, as Harold moved more in the direction of field independence, her style became increasingly mismatched to his.

Harold's partners' preferred styles were probably field independent, and he became increasingly mismatched to them as his field sensitive interests resurfaced. The mismatch was the company. His interests in computer graphics were beginning to show that he was "field sensitive in field independent clothing." Actually Harold had the potential to be a balanced bicognitive. At the time he came to therapy he was in a state of mismatch in different aspects of his life: he needed to be field sensitive in his behavior at home and to recognize his resurgent field sensitive interests in the domain of work and career.

Analysis of Cultural Mismatch

Harold's preferred cultural orientation was modernistic-urban, but he did acquire some traditional values from his parents, particularly in the gender role and interpersonal domains.

Jan's cultural orientation was semi-urban traditional.

Harold's partners had all been reared in cities on the East Coast of the United States, so they were more oriented to the modern-urban style than Harold was.

General Clinical Considerations. Harold should be assessed for antianxiety medication. He also needs to learn stress reduction techniques in order to manage his stress more effectively.

Troy C.

Background. Troy was born and reared in a medium-sized, predominantly Anglo rural community in Central Texas. He was the youngest of three children. Troy's father was a career officer in the army, and his mother was an English grammar teacher in the high school in which Troy was enrolled.

Troy's parents both had very high expectations of him because his two older brothers failed to graduate from college. Since his early childhood, Troy's mother devoted a great deal of time in preparing him for school. When he started school, she tutored him and helped him with his homework.

Troy's father was close to the older children, but with Troy he was more distant and formal. Troy was not encouraged to participate with him in his two major hobbies—fishing and gardening.

Troy liked to read fiction as well as biographies and autobiographies. He had primarily been a loner through childhood and adolescence, and because the family lived in a predominantly middle class, Anglo neighborhood, other children his age did not socialize with him. Occasionally he visited with his cousins who lived in the African-American section of town.

In school Troy was the only African-American enrolled in enriched classes. His classmates, while friendly at school, rarely invited him to parties or functions held outside of school. Troy had tried to befriend other African-Americans in his school, but for the most part they labeled him as being rich, the son of a teacher, and perceived him as socializing primarily with Anglos.

Socialization and Life Experiences. Troy was socialized in a traditional rural community in Central Texas. Prior to age 10, he lived in an African-American neighborhood, surrounded by relatives. His early traditional socialization led to a preference for a field sensitive orientation. When his family moved to a predominantly Anglo neighborhood, however, he was exposed to a modern cultural environment. Most of Troy's early socialization was done by his mother, particularly in the areas of thinking and problem-solving.

For the most part Troy's classes were field independent in orientation, that is, their focus was on the memorization of details or on analytical thinking and on individual competition. Additionally, most of his classmates were field independent in orientation.

Pattern of Adjustment. At the time Troy was brought to therapy, his relationship with his mother was characterized by frustration and conflict. Having suppressed and repressed anger towards her, he now rebelled against her "pushiness." Troy did not respect his father because he did not perceive him as taking a strong stand against his mother. Troy would often act out in passive-aggressive ways towards his parents; he would forget tasks that he was asked to do around the house or he would procrastinate.

His relationship with his Anglo classmates was distant and formal. He was not included in the activities of his African-American schoolmates except on those occasions when they needed his help. To cope, Troy spent his free time in his room reading, writing poetry, and fantasizing.

Symptoms. Troy was retreating from reality and fantasized that he was an alien from another planet. He was isolated from his parents and his peers.

He said, "No one can understand me so I guess I'm really different, like, from another planet."

Analysis of Cognitive Styles Mismatch

Troy was preferred field sensitive in most domains, but when he attempted to tutor his African-American schoolmates, he adopted a field independent style, influenced by his mother's preferred teaching style.

Troy's parents were bicognitive-preferred field independents as were most of his Anglo classmates.

His African-American schoolmates were probably preferred field sensitive (at least in learning and problem-solving), responding negatively to Troy's field independent style of teaching.

Analysis of Cultural Mismatch

Troy had a partial bicultural orientation; that is, he was partially developed in both the traditional African-American and modern Anglo-rural mainstream cultures.

Troy's parents and brothers were preferred bicultural: They had both a traditional African-American and also a rural-modernistic Anglo orientation.

Troy's classmates were preferred modernistic-rural mainstream Anglo.

General Clinical Considerations. Troy needs to be evaluated to determine if his tendency to fantasize about being an alien is part of the symptom pattern of schizophrenia.

Wanda M.

Background. Wanda was one of two children. She and her older brother, Sam, were reared in a large city on the East Coast of the United States. Her father, a supervisor with the Postal Service, was an alcoholic. Her mother, a secretary in a law firm, fit the description of a codependent personality who inadvertently reinforced the addictive behaviors of her spouse. While Wanda's father was warm and attentive towards the family when he was drinking, he was irritable and distant when sober. Her mother was passive and, for the most part, emotionally uninvolved with the children.

Wanda and her brother, only one year apart in age, had very different personalities: Sam was preferred field sensitive, and rebellious towards his parents and other authority figures.

In school Wanda's favorite subjects were math and languages. She earned a masters in business administration from a large midwestern university and obtained a job with a state agency in California. While in this job, she met her husband, Javier, a Hispanic man who had grown up in a traditional Hispanic family in Southern California.

At the time Wanda sought therapy, she was in her early thirties and the mother of two children. She and Javier had been married for six years. She had recently taken a position as a manager in a large international corporation and was the only woman on her office management team.

Socialization and Life Experiences. Wanda grew up in a modernistic city; her home and neighborhood were modern-urban mainstream Anglo middle class. In her family, Wanda was forced into the role of "hero child," a well recognized role in many dysfunctional families. She was encouraged to behave in a bicognitive manner in the family setting—her parents needed her to be self-sufficient and to be the "perfect" child who could hold the family together. Her brother's acting out and his problems at school and with the law reinforced this role. Wanda was expected to be sensitive to the feelings of others and to give emotional support to the members of her family.

She was socialized into the field sensitive style in the interpersonal domain because this was her father's preferred style when he was drinking. In school Wanda was a leader because of her interests in different languages and cultures. She was elected president of the International Club and of the Spanish Club. Wanda continued these interests by concentrating on international business in college.

Pattern of Adjustment. When Wanda left for college, she began to establish her independence from her parents. She would talk to them on the phone only twice a year, write to them occasionally, and visit them rarely. Wanda was happy with the bicognitive demands of the MBA program.

Wanda was attracted to Javier because he was Hispanic and because he and his family spoke Spanish fluently. She was comfortable with his preferred field sensitive cognitive style, although she often had problems with his rural traditional orientation. Javier's preferred style and that of his family had an influence on Wanda. Because of her bicognitive orientation, she adopted a preferred field sensitive style in the early years of the marriage. However, once Wanda started to work at her new job, its demands encouraged her to adopt a field independent style to fit the competitive, male-oriented atmosphere. As she became more field independent in her style, Javier and the children began to complain about her, and the intimacy and closeness she had felt with them began to break down.

Symptoms. As Wanda became more field independent in her cognitive style, she became more and more uncomfortable. This reminded her of the "hero child" role her parents had expected her to play within the family. At work, she was also uncomfortable with the pettiness, competitiveness, and sexism of her male colleagues. She discovered that it was only when she had been drinking that she was able to tolerate them.

At home, drinking caused her to forget the problems at the office, and helped her to switch to the field sensitive style Javier and the children were accustomed to. She realized that the only time that she and Javier were intimate was when they had both been drinking.

When Wanda came to therapy, she was both confused and worried that her drinking was getting out of hand, especially in view of her father's alcoholism. She also feared that she was losing her closeness with the only security in her life—Javier and her children. She was afraid that she would be alone and that she was too "different" to be successful in either work or marriage. "I feel torn apart by the demands of my work and those of my family. I feel very confused and angry. I don't know what to do."

Cognitive Styles Mismatch

Wanda developed as a bicognitive, although her field sensitive and field independent styles remained separate (almost like two separate personalities), much as those of her father had been.

When she met Javier, Wanda felt that she had finally found someone with whom she could use her field sensitive style in the domain of home and family; however, as the demands of her job encouraged a field independent orientation, she began to be mismatched to Javier and her children.

Wanda was mismatched to her male colleagues at work, and at the time she sought counseling, she was somewhat uncomfortable when she had to adopt a field independent approach. She felt pushed into it much as she was when she had been a "hero child."

Cultural Styles Mismatch Analysis

Wanda was urban-modernistic in her cultural orientation, but grew up with a nostalgia for traditionalism which had been encouraged by the German-Irish background of her father, and by the stories of family and community celebrations he told when he was drinking. This fueled Wanda's interest in different cultures and languages and eventually led to her interest in international business.

Wanda was initially mismatched to her husband's urban-traditional Hispanic cultural orientation, but her nostalgia for this type of value system motivated her to accommodate herself to it.

She was also mismatched to the extreme urban-traditional orientation of her male colleagues and, in particular, to their individually competitive, sexist, sports-oriented, drinking culture.

Wanda was also mismatched with the traditional-urban value systems of the Hispanic, African-American, Asian and Anglo managers she supervised.

General Clinical Considerations. Wanda needs to be assessed for chemical dependency, compulsive and/or addictive behaviors, and referred to appropriate Alcoholics Anonymous, Adult Children of Alcoholics and Codependency meetings.

SUMMARY

The flex theory of personality helps to identify those areas of mismatch in the cultural and cognitive domains of life which lead to barriers in the development of multicultural personality styles. The analysis of the areas of mismatch suggests goals for psychotherapy. Cultural and cognitive mismatch analyses for Imelda, Harold, Troy, and Wanda helped to pinpoint the origins of the feelings of differentness and of the symptoms of the mismatch syndrome. Furthermore, the concepts of the flex theory of personality help to identify those areas of mismatch in the cultural and cognitive domains of life that interfere with the development of multicultural personalities and life styles. The therapeutic approach of choice for adjustment problems associated with mismatch is multicultural psychotherapy and/or counseling.

The focus of multicultural therapy is on the development of personality flex and multicultural orientations towards life. In addition, clients are given an awareness of how they have been the victims of mismatch shock and feelings of differentness. Clients are empowered to change the environment, helping to create a multicultural society sensitive to diversity, and oriented towards peace and cooperation.

The Flex Theory of Personality was applied to information obtained through the life histories of Imelda, Harold, Troy, and Wanda in order to understand how the mismatch syndrome developed in these clients. The life histories also helped to identify general clinical considerations as well as some of the goals to be addressed in multicultural therapy.

Chapter 5

The Multicultural Model of Psychotherapy and Counseling: An Overview

In the previous chapter, the principal concepts of the cognitive and cultural flex theory of personality were applied to show how Imelda, Harold, Troy, and Wanda were mismatched with people and institutions in their environments, and how mismatch was associated with feelings of differentness, alienation, and despair.

This chapter introduces an approach to psychotherapy and counseling which evolved from the experience of treating clients who, like Imelda, Harold, Troy, and Wanda, were the victims of feeling different, and of mismatch shock.

The Multicultural Model of Psychotherapy and Counseling differs from other treatment approaches in several ways:

1. It views every client as having the potential for multicultural development. It encourages the therapist or counselor to respect clients' origins as reflected in unique cultural and cognitive styles, because these serve as the foundation for multicultural development and for the development of maximum potential in the personality (Maslow, 1954).

2. It views the therapist as also having preferred cognitive and cultural styles. It encourages therapists and counselors to become aware of their own unique cultural and cognitive styles, and to learn how to flex in order to best match the unique styles of clients.

3. The therapist or counselor makes use of the opportunities for multicultural growth offered by a diverse society, and in the process of therapy, encourages the client to take diversity challenges which promote growth.

4. Clients are encouraged to become active change agents not only to

enhance their own multicultural development, but also to help develop a society of social justice, peace, and cooperation which will be responsive and sensitive to the individual differences of all its citizens.

TASKS OF THE MULTICULTURAL THERAPIST

Specifically, the multicultural therapist or counselor has seven major tasks in therapy, outlined as follows:

Matching Clients in an Atmosphere of Acceptance

The therapist provides a non-judgmental, positive, accepting atmosphere devoid of conformity or assimilation pressures. In this climate, clients feel free to express their uniqueness in the form of their preferred cognitive and cultural styles. This accomplishes several objectives:

1. It helps clients overcome feelings of differentness and of mismatch shock which negatively affect their adjustment, and prevent openness to multicultural development.

2. It allows clients to abandon the false self and to express his or her unique self, thus allowing the therapist to know how best to match the preferred styles of the client. This helps the client to feel validated and accepted.

The therapist continues to match the client to further eliminate the effects of the mismatch syndrome, and to continue to gain the client's trust. The most important initial area of match is communication style, as it is important for the client to feel totally understood by the therapist. Continued match procedures gain the trust of the client by reducing alienation. Matching also helps in the assessment of clients' preferred styles as the false self recedes and the unique self emerges. Additionally, matching by the therapist helps to remove those barriers to learning from diversity that have kept clients from achieving their multicultural potential.

Making a Formal Assessment of the Client's Preferred Styles

As a cross-check on the assessment done through observations, the therapist or counselor administers three personality inventories which assess the client's preferred cognitive and cultural styles. These inventories accomplish three goals:

1.   They indicate how well behavioral observations match the client's self report of preferred styles.

2.   They provide materials for discussion of important therapeutic issues.

3.   When the findings of the assessment are shared with clients, they can participate in goal setting and gain a first-hand understanding of the unique self reflected in their preferred styles.

Conducting a Life History Interview with the Client

The life history interview with the client (discussed in detail in chapter 7) identifies a time or times in the client's life (as in the case of Harold) when the pressure to conform or assimilate caused a suppression of a preferred style. The life history helps to identify those people and institutions to which the client has felt most matched and mismatched. It also helps to isolate barriers to multicultural development such as Imelda's strong negative feelings towards mainstream Anglo-Americans, and Troy's alienation from his African-American peers.

In addition, the life history interview helps to identify personality building blocks that can be used in multicultural development. An example is the discovery of Wanda's long-standing interest in cultures with a strong sense of family unity.

Finally, the life history interview helps to survey the resources and potential opportunities present in the client's environment that could facilitate multicultural development.

Making a Self-Assessment

In multicultural therapy it is necessary that the therapist or counselor evaluate his or her own preferred styles to determine areas of match and mismatch with the client, requiring the therapist to flex in order to better match the client.

This self-assessment is important to determine whether the therapist has a sufficient range of flex to provide an adequate match to the client's preferred styles. It also helps the therapist identify his or her biases, prejudices, and preferences. In this way, it can be ascertained whether there are any stereotypes or negative attitudes that might interfere with establishment of rapport.

Finally, self-assessment provides therapists and counselors with an opportunity to identify those areas of cognitive and cultural style in which they will need additional multicultural development.

Introducing the Client to Cognitive and Cultural Flex and the Multicultural Model

The client's active participation in therapy is an important component of this model. For this reason, the therapist or counselor introduces the client to the major concepts of both the flex theory of personality and the Multicultural Model of Psychotherapy.

Clients' knowledge and awareness of these concepts enables him or her to monitor progress. Clients also become more invested in the success of therapy during the process of setting personal goals. In the larger scheme, clients' involvement empowers them to become agents of change.

Introducing mismatch to the client's preferred cultural and cognitive styles is the beginning of the development of cultural and cognitive flex. This introduction is done in the context of match. The client is encouraged to participate in social situations and relationships which can foster the development of new cultural and cognitive styles.

Mismatch is practiced in the safe atmosphere of therapy through the writing of scripts and role-playing. This practice serves to develop cognitive and cultural flex as well as to encourage the client to learn how to empathize with people whose cultural and cognitive styles differ from his or her own.

Through the use of homework assignments clients try out scripts in the world outside the therapy room and evaluate their own progress in these efforts. This phase continues the development of cognitive and cultural flex as well as the development of clients' preferred styles. Further, clients develop self-confidence in interacting with people and situations which require the use of styles different from their own.

To assess the progress of clients as they proceed through the therapy, the therapist makes continued observations of the clients during sessions, noting progress on the Preferred Cognitive and Cultural Styles and Observation Checklists. Scores are compared to those ratings made by the therapist in the initial stages of therapy to note the degree of change.

This ongoing comparison helps the therapist determine the degree of progress on the goals established for therapy and helps clients to see how much progress they are making as therapy proceeds. The comparison also enable the therapist and clients to develop new goals or to modify existing ones.

Assessing the Client's Progress in Flex Development

Once the mismatch phase of therapy is well under way, the therapist assesses client progress in the different domains of cultural and cognitive styles. The data obtained from readministration of the paper and pencil inventories and from the observation instruments are compared to those obtained in the initial stage of therapy. These comparisons help to determine whether it will be necessary to make changes in the therapeutic plan. Feedback to the client assures continued involvement and commitment to the goals of multicultural therapy and counseling.

Encouraging the Client to Become a Change Agent

Clients learn how to encourage changes in the environment in order to ensure the best match to their preferred styles from others and from those institutions and agencies which most affect their daily lives. Clients also learn how to become peer counselors for those who are suffering from feeling different and from mismatch shock. In addition, they learn how to become multicultural ambassadors, facilitating the development of a multicultural society.

Transforming clients into change agents empowers them to gain control over their destiny. Also, clients become more committed to multiculturalism by helping other victims of mismatch. Working to introduce other individuals and institutions to the advantages and benefits of multiculturalism helps to promote the development of a society of peace and cooperation stimulating the maximum development of the individual potential of all its citizens.

GOALS OF MULTICULTURAL PSYCHOTHERAPY AND COUNSELING

The Multicultural Model of Psychotherapy and Counseling has four major goals: to reduce mismatch shock; to help clients recognize and accept their unique selves; to help clients to achieve cultural and cognitive flex; and to empower clients to change the environment and to become advocates for a multicultural society.

Overcoming the Mismatch Syndrome

The first goal of multicultural therapy is to reduce alienation and feelings of helplessness and despair. As long as clients suffer from the negative effects of mismatch, they cannot learn from other people and groups who are different. They are unable to discover their unique selves and to develop that uniqueness to its fullest.

A person in mismatch shock cannot take full advantage of opportunities offered by a multicultural society. Mismatch shock closes experience and learning filters, causing clients to repeat old behaviors, attitudes, and values which have led to failure in the past.

Recognizing and Accepting the Unique Self

The client in mismatch shock has serious identity problems. The "tyranny of the shoulds," reflected in the conformist and assimilationist approaches of society, forces the client to reject the unique self in favor of a false self.

Multicultural therapy first helps clients identify the self they may have suppressed earlier in life and to recognize how pressures from others and/or from society have forced them to try to be someone other than the unique self. This makes clients aware of how they became victims of conformity and/or assimilation.

Multicultural therapy then helps clients to accept themselves and develop to the fullest extent possible by learning how to flex cognitively and culturally.

Achieving Cognitive and Cultural Flex

Once clients accept the unique self and understand how mismatch has led to alienation and unhappiness, and once they recognize the advantages offered by a multicultural society to personal development, multicultural therapy approaches proceed to help in the development of cultural and cognitive flexibility which facilitate the development and expression of the unique self.

Empowering Clients to Become Change Agents, Peer Counselors and Multicultural Ambassadors

The multicultural model of psychotherapy teaches clients the concepts and procedures of the flex theory of personality and the Multicultural Model of Therapy so that they can create change in their environment. By encouraging the environment to become more sensitive to diversity, clients ensure a better match for their unique styles as well as for the unique styles of others. Empowerment also encourages clients to become multicultural peer counselors and ambassadors for the development of a cooperative and peaceful multicultural society.

These four major goals are dependent upon the accomplishment of a series of subgoals. The first two subgoals are accomplished by identifying the relationships of pressures to conform and assimilate to choice of cultural and cognitive styles. The life history also provides an opportunity for clients to identify possible attitudes and values associated with ethnocentrism and the development of negative stereotypes which have prevented them from participating in and learning from diversity. The goals and subgoals identified here can be accomplished by following the steps of multicultural therapy. The therapeutic process generally consists of seventeen sessions. Each session focuses on specific goals. These include:

1.   Helping clients recognize that they have been victims of the pressures to conform and assimilate, a product of the "tyranny of the shoulds."

2.   Helping clients to overcome potential barriers standing in the way of multicultural development. First, clients have to become aware of forces and factors in their histories which may have resulted in closing learning-experience filters, and in an adherence to rigid cognitive and cultural styles which have isolated them from diversity and have resulted in alienation. Closed learning-experience filters are usually associated with ethnocentric attitudes and with negative stereotypes of those who are different from oneself.

3.   Encouraging clients to try out new values, world views, and cognitive styles in the safe environment of match provided in the therapeutic setting and relationship. This initial experience with match helps clients to eliminate barriers which have blocked their multicultural development. It also motivates and prepares clients to participate in diversity challenges which can give them the opportunity to develop the cultural and cognitive flex essential to multicultural personality development.

4.   Helping clients learn the strategies and concepts of both the flex theory of personality and the Multicultural Model of Therapy can make them active change agents so that people and institutions around them can better match their unique styles as well as those of other citizens. The therapist also empowers clients to become multicultural educators, peer counselors, and ambassadors.

SESSION-BY-SESSION DESCRIPTION WITH A FOCUS ON THERAPY GOALS

Session 1:

The first session lasts about 90 minutes and focuses on the development of an atmosphere of acceptance and respect, encouraging the expression of clients' unique selves through their preferred cultural and cognitive styles.

During this session the therapist or counselor must keep in mind that because of the effects of pressures to conform and mismatch shock, the client may not initially be open to self-expression.

It is during the initial session that the therapist performs a preliminary assessment of the unique self through observation of the cultural and cognitive styles of the client. The therapist also begins to match and to monitor the effects of match on the client using behavior observation check lists.

The therapist administers the Traditionalism-Modernism Instrument, the BOLS, and the Family Attitudes Scale to the client. While the client is completing the instruments, the therapist examines his or her self-observations and compares them to ratings of the client's preferred cultural and cognitive styles. The therapist then determines whether he or she posesses the range of flex which will be required to maximize the chances for success with the client, or whether the client should be referred to another therapist.

Session 2:

In the course of the second session, the therapist or counselor continues to match the client and does a brief life history. During this session the therapist explains the principal concepts of the flex theory of personality and offers feedback on the results of the assessment instruments the client completed during the initial session. It is during the second session that the therapist and the client set the goals for therapy. The second session is approximately 75 minutes in length.

Sessions 3 and 4:

While the therapist continues to match the client's preferred cultural and cognitive styles, he or she obtains a more detailed life history from the client with a focus on match and mismatch. The therapist introduces script writing exercises and empathy projection.

During these sessions there is continued discussion of the principal concepts of the Flex Model as well as discussion of the possible diversity challenges available to the client. At this time, the therapist attempts to reduce any negative stereotypes and possible negative attitudes towards diversity.

Sessions 5 through 10:

While continuing to match the client's preferred styles, the therapist introduces mismatch through match using script writing, empathy projec-

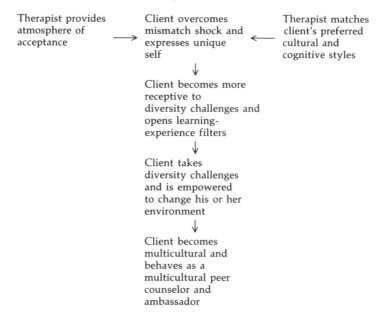

Flow Chart of Multicultural Model

| Therapist provides atmosphere of acceptance | → | Client overcomes mismatch shock and expresses unique self | ← | Therapist matches client's preferred cultural and cognitive styles |

↓

Client becomes more receptive to diversity challenges and opens learning-experience filters

↓

Client takes diversity challenges and is empowered to change his or her environment

↓

Client becomes multicultural and behaves as a multicultural peer counselor and ambassador

FIGURE 5.1: Major Stages of Multilcultural Model of
Psychotherapy and Counseling

tion, role playing, and diversity challenges during the sessions as well as in homework assignments.

Sessions 11 through 15:

Session 11 is used to assess the progress of the development of flexibility. The remaining sessions of this phase are used to work on areas of flex not yet mastered. It is during these later sessions that the client is introduced to the role of change agent, multicultural peer counselor, and multicultural ambassador. Session 15 focuses on assessing the progress of the growth of the client in these areas. Depending on the client's progress more sessions may be scheduled, otherwise, regularly scheduled therapy sessions are terminated at this point.

Session 16:

Six months after the last regularly scheduled session, the client and therapist meet to follow up and plan additional sessions if necessary.

Session 17:

Six months after session 16 or after the final session of the series of sessions planned after session 16, the client and therapist meet for an additional follow-up and to evaluate the need for additional sessions. Sessions 3 through 17 are approximately 50 minutes in length. Figure 5.1 summarizes the major stages of the Multicultural Model of Psychotherapy and Counseling.

SUMMARY

The Multicultural Model of Psychotherapy and Counseling evolved from the experience of doing therapy and counseling with clients who were victims of feeling different and who were suffering from the symptoms of the mismatch syndrome. The model is a unique treatment approach which views every client and therapist as having the potential for becoming multicultural, and for fostering the development of a multicultural society. This chapter presented the major concepts, tasks, and goals of the Multicultural Model of Psychotherapy.

Chapter 6
The Therapist

Most psychotherapy and counseling models ignore the powerful impact that the therapist's personality has on the outcome of therapy. Witkin and Goodenough (1977) showed that the preferred cognitive style of therapists seemed to be reflected in their therapeutic styles. For example, therapists who were preferred field independent tended to talk less and to be less directive in therapy than their field sensitive colleagues.

The cultural styles of therapists have also been found to be important in mental health service delivery for the "different" (Torrey, 1973; Sue, 1981). When therapists and clients share the same cultural world view and the same values, therapy is more effective.

Focus on the therapist's preferred styles and on the degree of match between the cognitive and cultural styles of the therapist and the client are of central importance to the multicultural model of psychotherapy. When the therapist matches the client, mismatch shock and the feeling of being different are reduced. This increases the client's trust and feelings of self-efficacy which in turn increase the willingness to explore diversity and to learn from it by opening up learning experience filters.

This chapter focuses on the preferred cultural and cognitive styles of the therapist. Further, it examines the degree to which the therapist can and should flex in order to match the client and serve as a multicultural model.

THE THERAPIST AS A PRODUCT OF HISTORY

The therapist's preferred cultural and cognitive styles and degree of flex have been shaped by personal history vis-a-vis diversity. Thus, therapists need a systematic approach for determining how their preferred styles and abilities to flex have been shaped by socialization and life experiences. One technique for learning this is through a self life history.

The Self Life History

The following sample questions can serve as a general guideline for developing a self life history:

1. How much cognitive and cultural diversity was reflected in the make-up of my nuclear and extended families? (Were parents, blood relatives, and relatives by marriage with whom I interacted extensively as a child or an adolescent members of different ethnic, racial, religious, regional, or socioeconomic groups? Did they represent different values, ideologies, and philosophies of life? Did they represent different cognitive style preferences?)
2. How cognitively and culturally diverse were the countries, communities, and neighborhoods in which I grew up and in which I have lived?
3. How diverse were the students and staff populations of the schools I attended?
4. How diverse were the coaches, music teachers, scout masters, job supervisors, clergy, and other influential authority figures?
5. How diverse were the people I dated or those I considered to be close friends?
6. How diverse were the places—homes, communities, regions, countries—I visited?
7. How much diversity was reflected in the courses I had in college and in graduate school? The novels, biographies, and autobiographies I have read?
8. How much diversity is represented in my hobbies and pastimes?
9. What is the nature and the frequency of the diversity challenges I have undertaken?

Information gained by answering such questions as these provides a good indication of the therapist's attitudes towards diversity. These questions also help to inventory the size and heterogeneity of the pool of personality resources (see chapter 3) the therapist has available for cultural and cognitive flex in therapy and counseling.

In addition to the self life history, therapists can do self-assessments of their preferred cultural styles and of the degree of their capability to flex in these two domains. The assessment instruments described below and provided in the appendix of this book can be used for this purpose.

Self-Assessment of Cultural Flex

The Multicultural Experience Inventory (appendix A) is a tool which can be used for the assessment of cultural flex. This instrument provides an indication of the degree of exposure the therapist has had to diversity in the past, as well as to the degree to which he or she is exposed to diversity in the present.

The Traditionalism-Modernism Inventory (appendix B) is a scale which assesses the degree of identification with traditional and modern values and belief systems. This instrument yields a score indicating the degree of agreement with traditional or modern values, as well as indicating the degree of flexibility; that is, the degree of identification with both sets of values and belief systems.

Both the Multicultural Experience Inventory and the Traditionalism-Modernism Inventory can be used in still another way to assess the therapist's degree of cultural flex. Immediately upon concluding a therapeutic session, the therapist can review the items of the instruments and place check marks by those which were related to interpretations she or he made in the course of a therapy session. The therapist can also check her or his own responses to the items with those made by the client to gauge the degree of match or mismatch with the client.

Self-Assessment of Cognitive Flex

Therapists are also encouraged to assess their cognitive style preference and the degree to which they can flex cognitively by doing a self-assessment with the Therapist's Cognitive Styles Observation Checklist and with the Bicognitive Orientation to Life Scale.

Therapist Cognitive Styles Observation Checklist. This instrument is used in much the same way as the Cognitive Styles Observation Checklist described in chapter 7. The following are the field sensitive and field independent therapist behaviors which have been identified:

Communication Style

Field Sensitive

_____ 1. The therapist does more talking than the client during the session.

_____ 2. The therapist personalizes communications; is self-disclosing.

_____ 3. The therapist uses both verbal and non-verbal modes of communication.

Field Independent

_____ 1. The therapist talks less than the client during the session.

_____ 2. The therapist remains a "blank screen" for the client.

_____ 3. The therapist emphasizes verbal communication.

Interpersonal Relationship Style

Field Sensitive

_____ 1. The therapist is informal and establishes a close personal relationship with the client.

_____ 2. The therapist focuses on the nature of the therapist-client relationship in therapy.

Field Independent

_____ 1. The therapist is formal and maintains "professional" distance.

_____ 2. The therapist emphasizes self-reliance and is problem-focused.

Motivational Styles

Field Sensitive

_____ 1. The therapist emphasizes social rewards to the client.

_____ 2. The therapist emphasizes achievement for others as one of the goals of therapy.

Field Independent

_____ 1. The therapist emphasizes self-rewards.

_____ 2. The therapist emphasizes achievement for self.

Therapeutic-Teaching Styles

Field Sensitive

_____ 1. The therapist becomes a model for the client in teaching new behaviors, values, and perspectives.

_____ 2. The therapist uses direct interpretation.

_____ 3. The therapist uses a deductive approach (global to specific) to teaching in therapy.

Field Independent

_____ 1. The therapist uses the discovery approach.

_____ 2. The therapist uses reflection, encouraging clients to arrive at their own interpretations.

_____ 3. The therapist uses an inductive (specific to global) approach to teaching in therapy.

The Therapist Cognitive Styles Observation Checklist is provided in appendix C to facilitate duplication for use by therapists and counselors.

By keeping this instrument in front of them during the course of therapy, therapists can monitor personal behaviors used frequently in the sessions and then check these against observations made of the client's behavior. A comparison of the two identifies areas of match and mismatch.

The BOLS (appendix D) is an instrument which assesses the degree of preference for field independent or field sensitive cognitive styles as well as the degree of cognitive flex.

BECOMING A FLEXIBLE THERAPIST

It is important for the therapist to keep in mind that cultural and cognitive flex are processes, and not fixed personality characteristics. Therefore, therapists should consider themselves as always being in the process of moving toward, but never reaching, the goal of total cognitive and cultural flexibility.

Because flexibility is constantly in process, it is important for therapists to work continuously toward the development of cultural and cognitive flex by using some of the same procedures and techniques they use with their clients. These will be described in more detail in chapters that follow, but they are introduced here with a brief discussion focusing on development of the therapist's flexibility.

Empathy

Viewing the world through the eyes of someone whose cultural and/or cognitive style is very different from the therapist's is an exercise for developing flex. The procedure which can be used is what is referred to as *empathy projection* — trying to understand the point of view and the feelings of someone whose values and cognitive styles may be very different from those of the therapist.

A good place to start is with loved ones, family members, friends, and colleagues whose values and cognitive styles are different from the preferred styles of the therapist. Another approach is to read the biographies and autobiographies of people whose cultures and values are different from the preferred styles of the therapist. (A list of biographies, autobiographies, and novels written by authors of various ethnic or racial groups is included in the Selected Readings section.)

Script Writing and Role-playing

Focusing on someone they know well, therapists should develop scripts which attempt to match that person, role-playing the script with friends, and then trying out the script with the person whom they want to match. After trying out the script, therapists can evaluate themselves by using the homework effectiveness assessment instrument described in chapter 8 and provided in appendix F, and by reviewing the categories of the Cognitive Style Behavior Observation Instrument. Therapists can then rewrite the script and make another attempt if necessary.

Modeling

Therapists can make changes in their friendship patterns in order to have opportunities to interact with people who have cognitive and cultural styles different from their own. By observing and then modeling the behaviors and values that they observe and by attempting to communicate and relate effectively to these new friends, therapists can learn unfamiliar cognitive and cultural styles.

Diversity Challenges

Therapists can try out new tasks and activities or hobbies in order to create diversity challenges. Making new friendships can also stimulate the development of cultural and cognitive style flex.

Travel

Therapists can broaden cultural and cognitive horizons by visiting different neighborhoods or communities in their immediate area as well as by traveling to different regions or countries in order to gain familiarity with other styles and perspectives on life.

LIMITS TO THERAPIST FLEX

There are limits to the extent to which the therapist or counselor should attempt to flex in order to match clients, and these fall into two major categories:

1. Every therapist has an effectiveness-comfort range of flex within which she or he can match clients while feeling comfortable, genuine, and effective.
2. There are limits imposed by moral and ethical considerations—it would not be appropriate to match the client in situations in which matching would reinforce the client's pathology.

The Effectiveness-comfort Range

Each therapist needs to become familiar with her or his effectiveness-comfort range through experience and self-evaluation. The greater the diversity of the therapist's case load, the greater the opportunities for self-evaluation under different conditions of match. Therapists should take the following issues into consideration when they are in the process of determining the extent of their effectiveness-comfort range:

1. *Therapy goals* — The therapist needs to be cognizant of the match requirements of the goals which have been established for the client. The therapist, through experience, comes to recognize that certain client goals require complete shifts in style during the course of therapy: A client who is suffering from a Post-traumatic Stress Disorder for example, may require a field sensitive match in the initial stages and a predominant field independent orientation in the later stages of therapy. Thus, when the therapist and client develop the goals of therapy in the second session, the therapist needs to decide whether or not he or she will have the required range of flex to meet the client's needs during the entire course of treatment. If the demands required by the therapeutic plan can not be met, then the therapist must be prepared to refer the client to another professional who might have the range of flex required to work effectively with that client.

2. *Limit-setting and confrontation* — Some clients, such as Borderline and Antisocial Personality Disorders, may require the establishment of firm limits and the use of confrontation (behaviors typical of a field independent therapy orientation) during the course of therapy. Therapists must know if their effectiveness-comfort range will allow them to be comfortable and genuine with limit setting and confrontation.

3. *Structure* — Some clients, such as Oppositional and Conduct Disorders, may require a very structured type of therapy, one that is typical of an extreme field independent type of therapeutic style. The therapists must ask themselves how comfortable and effective they can be in employing a structured approach to treatment.

4. *Empathy* — Clients who have been physically and/or sexually abused may require strong and deep empathy. Therapists must determine if their effectiveness-comfort range will permit the degree of field sensitive orientation in therapy required by victims of abuse.

Moral and Ethical Issues

The therapist or counselor needs to be cognizant of the fact that in some situations matching behavior may be inadvertently interpreted by the client as support for pathological behavior. This is particularly difficult in cases in which clients need to establish good rapport with the therapist before they can gain the confidence they need to initiate cognitive and cultural style changes. Matching needs to be done with the clear message to the client that it does not imply approval of values and life styles which are potentially damaging to the client or to others. Another area of therapy in which moral and ethical issues are paramount concerns the degree to which the client should be encouraged by the therapist to develop unfamiliar styles. Clients, like therapists, have ranges of flex within which they feel comfortable at certain stages in their lives. The therapist needs to be cognizant of the fact that at certain stages in their lives, clients may be unable to develop the degree of flex which will lead to perfect balance. For example, encouraging Imelda in the direction of an extreme modernistic and field independent style could have resulted in the greater alienation of members of her family and her peers. The therapist had to consider that she was living in a traditional community, emphasizing traditional values and a field sensitive orientation to life. Once Imelda leaves her home community to attend the state university, located in a community more representative of modern values and field independent styles, it may become easier for her to further explore the development of the field independent and modernistic domains of her personality. Thus, in determining the degree of flexibility of both therapist and client, it is important not to loose sight of the principal paradigm on which the Multicultural Model is based—multicultural person-environment fit.

SUMMARY

Therapists, like clients, are the products of their socialization histories and life experiences. The Multicultural Model of psychotherapy requires that the therapist as well as the client be cognizant of preferred cultural and cognitive styles reflected in behaviors, thinking patterns, and life styles.

Therapists are encouraged to do short self-life histories and self-assessments using the same instruments they use to assess preferred styles and degree of flex in clients. Therapists are also asked to use the same techniques and procedures employed to encourage the development of flex in clients so that they too can develop greater flex and thereby become more effective with a wider variety of clients.

There are, however, limits to which the therapist can and should flex to match clients. Therapists should not match the values of clients whose actions clearly threaten the lives or the well-being of themselves or others. It is the therapists themselves who must be the ultimate judges of the limits of their willingness and ability to match certain clients. They need to be aware of how entrenched they are with respect to preferred cognitive and cultural styles. Therapists must know when the demands of match would carry them beyond a range in which they feel comfortable, genuine, and effective.

Chapter 7

The First Stage of Multicultural Therapy and Counseling: Matching the Client's Preferred Styles

The principal goal of the first two sessions of multicultural psychotherapy and counseling is to match the preferred cultural and cognitive styles of the client. During the course of the first session the therapist establishes an atmosphere of nonjudgemental acceptance in which the client can begin to overcome the effects of the mismatch syndrome, and to express the unique self. The therapist then proceeds to match the client's preferred cultural and cognitive styles. In the second session, the therapist continues to match the client's preferred styles. In addition, a short life history is done with the client. It is also during the second session that the therapist or counselor introduces the client to the flex theory of personality and gives the client feedback concerning the findings of the assessment done in the first session in preparation for identifying the principal goals to be addressed in therapy.

THE INITIAL SESSION

The therapist establishes an atmosphere of nonjudgemental acceptance and begins the process of client assessment in the initial session. It is during this session that the client explains why therapy is being sought and what the client hopes to gain from it, while the therapist describes what the client can realistically expect and what the general course of therapy will be.

In this first session the therapist evaluates the client both casually through observation, and more formally through evaluation instruments.

Categorizing Initial Observations of Cultural Styles

The professional can gain early clues to the preferred style of the client from informal observations. The client who has a traditional orientation is likely to be dressed formally and may initially appear to be self-conscious, or even shy. The client who is more oriented towards a modern system of values on the other hand, is likely to be dressed more casually, with a behavior more reflective of self-confidence.

While the traditionally oriented client is deferential and likely to address the therapist by using the appropriate title, the modernistic client usually tries to relate to the therapist as an equal, and may use the therapist's first name, or at least inquire whether it is acceptable to do so.

The client with a traditional orientation will often expect the therapist to take the lead in therapy, expecting that the therapist will do most of the talking in the initial stages of the first session. The client with a modern orientation is likely to begin talking without encouragement from the therapist.

The client with a traditional orientation is usually sensitive to the social environment, and may comment on how the therapist's office looks or on particular items in it. The modernistically oriented client is usually inattentive to the social environment and to any nonverbal cues the therapist may project.

When explaining why therapy is sought, the traditionally oriented client will usually focus on relationships with intimate partners, family members, peers, colleagues, or others. The modernistic client, however, is more self-focused, emphasizing self-efficacy rather than interpersonal relationships.

Of course, not all clients fall clearly and totally into one category or the other. Clients with a mixed traditional and modern orientation will exhibit behaviors associated with both cultural styles. For example, a culturally flexible client could be self-confident and assertive in the session while at the same time indicating that therapy is sought because of a need to improve personal relationships.

The Preferred Cultural Styles Observation Checklist is an instrument comprised of behaviors which have been found (Ramirez, 1983) to be typical of clients with either modern or traditional orientations. It is useful in helping the therapist or counselor define the client's orientation. With the checklist in front of the therapist during the initial session, appropriate checks and notes can be made.

Typical observations from the checklist include the following:

Traditional	Modern
_____ behaves deferentially towards the therapist	_____ seeks to establish equal status with therapist
_____ expects the therapist to do most of the talking	_____ does most of the talking
_____ appears shy and self-controlling	_____ appears assertive and self-confident
_____ is observant of social environment	_____ seems to ignore social environment
_____ focuses on important others in relating reason(s) for seeking therapy	_____ focuses on self in relating reason(s) for seeking therapy

The Preferred Cultural Styles Observation Checklist is provided in appendix G to facilitate duplication for use by the therapists and counselors.

Manifestation of Preferred Cultural Styles in Case Studies

The cases presented earlier—those of Imelda, Harold, Troy, and Wanda—reflected a variety of preferred cultural styles.

Imelda. Imelda's traditional values were reflected in her manner of dress and in the way she related to the therapist. She was neatly dressed in a sport shirt and dress slacks, and wore her school jacket with a prominent athletic letter. Imelda was self-conscious at first, and avoided making eye contact with the therapist. She was deferential and respectful, referring to the therapist as "Doctor" and "Sir."

Harold. This client's strong modern orientation was reflected in his air of self-confidence and assertiveness. He walked into the therapist's office holding a note pad and pen. Harold started talking before the therapist had an opportunity to be seated.

When the therapist addressed him by his surname, he responded by saying, "Please call me Harold. May I call you Manuel?" He then announced he had a number of questions and proceeded to read these from his note pad. When he addressed the reasons for coming to therapy, Harold focused on his concerns about self-efficacy. It was obvious that his goal of improving relationships with significant others was secondary to that of feeling effective and creative again.

Troy. Troy's traditional values were revealed by the fact that he was self-conscious and quiet when his parents were in the therapy room with him. The therapist also noted that he wore a T-shirt with the name of a state university and the Greek letters of a fraternity.

After Troy's parents left the room at the therapist's request, Troy was deferent, referring to the therapist by his title. He spoke in a soft voice. When asked why he thought his parents had brought him to therapy, Troy talked about how he was unable to relate to them and to his peers, both African-American and Anglo, in school.

Troy's modernism became apparent in that he did most of the talking when he was alone with the therapist. His assertiveness was also reflected in his curiosity to know what the therapy would involve.

Wanda. Like Troy, Wanda had a mixed values and beliefs system. Her mix, however, was apparent in several domains. Like Harold, she was self-confident and assertive, but she addressed the therapist by his title and seemed to prefer to be addressed by her surname.

Wanda did not take a seat until the therapist was settled in his chair, but she did ask permission to take notes in the session, and had made a few notes on the topics she wanted to discuss prior to coming to the session. Wanda's modernism was expressed in her talkativeness, while her traditionalism was reflected in comments she made regarding the art displayed on the walls of the therapist's office, and about her knowledge of Hispanic cultures. Wanda seemed to give equal importance to her own need to be successful in her career and her need to feel closer to her husband, children, and professional colleagues, thus reflecting a traditional orientation in her reasons for seeking therapy.

Initial Match of Preferred Cultural Style

The therapist made an effort to match the preferred cultural style of each of the clients described in the case studies. Based on understandings gained in initial interactions with each client, the therapist sought to avoid mismatch.

Imelda. The therapist addressed the client by her surname. The therapist also showed respect for her shyness by using a soothing tone of voice and by projecting acceptance and concern through his body posture.

The therapist took the cue from Imelda that she wished him to be directive, so he began by mentioning the athletic letter on her jacket, opening a discussion about her involvement in basketball and volleyball at school. She gradually approached her problems as she talked about her teammates and teachers, her boyfriend, parents, and grandparents.

Harold. The therapist permitted Harold to address him by his first name and did the same when addressing the client. Following Harold's lead, the therapist took a note pad and pen and began taking notes as Harold spoke. The therapist also followed Harold's focus on self-efficacy when describing the reasons for seeking therapy, and indicated how the therapeutic approach he used might help in understanding and resolving the problems Harold was discussing.

Troy. The therapist respected Troy's traditional orientation in the presence of his parents, waiting until they were alone to ask questions of him. When the therapist addressed him by his surname, Troy asked to be addressed by his first name while continuing to use the therapist's title and surname in addressing him. When Troy became assertive and began to express his feelings, the therapist reinforced him through verbal and nonverbal cues.

Wanda. The therapist matched the modernism reflected in Wanda's assertiveness in therapy. He was also sensitive to the traditionalism reflected in her focus on improving her relationships with her family and colleagues. The therapist encouraged the traditional values evidenced in Wanda's desire to establish common interests with the therapist by way of the artwork displayed in his office, and through their knowledge of Hispanic cultures.

Categorizing Initial Observations of Cognitive Styles

Field Sensitive Cognitive Styles Preference and Client Behavior. The client whose preferred cognitive style is field sensitive usually communicates using both verbal and nonverbal modes. Facial expression, body posture, and tone of voice are likely to be just as important as what is said.

The client who is predominantly field sensitive also tends to give a global, or general, description of problems, and is likely to talk about relationships with others. The preferred field sensitive client gives the therapist the message that direction is welcome: "Where do I begin?"

Field Independent Cognitive Style Preference and Client Behavior. The preferred field independent style client follows a rather strict verbal mode of communication, selecting words carefully. Problems are usually described in detail, with the definitions of problems circumscribed.

Further, the client who is preferred field independent views problems as separate from the totality of being: "I just want some help with my lack of patience." The field independent client will usually initiate discussion in therapy and may even discuss hypotheses he or she has formed about problems: "I've been thinking, and I feel that the reason I don't have much patience is that I can't seem to relax."

Bicognition and Client Behavior. The client who can flex cognitively will use a mix of behaviors and approaches typical of both field independent and field sensitive clients. For example, a client who can flex cognitively may demonstrate a global view of problems but use an exclusively verbal communication mode.

The Preferred Cognitive Styles Observation Checklist

As for the case of the Preferred Cultural Styles Observation Checklist, the checklist for preferred cognitive styles evolved from research (Ramirez, 1983) with field sensitive and field independent subjects. As with the checklist for cultural styles, the therapist can keep the Preferred Cognitive Styles Observation Checklist in front of him or her during the course of the initial session in order to make check marks or notes based on observations of the client's behavior. The following are samples for the checklist for preferred cognitive styles:

Field Sensitive	Field Independent
_____ is self-disclosing	_____ depersonalizes problems
_____ shows interest in personalizing relationship with therapist	_____ relationship with therapist secondary to focus on problems to be addressed in therapy
_____ indicates that social rewards from therapist will be important to progress	_____ indicates that increase in personal well-being will be important to progress
_____ global focus and deductive learning style	_____ detail-focused and inductive (specific-to-global) learning style

The Preferred Cognitive Styles Checklist is provided in appendix H to facilitate duplication for use by therapists and counselors.

Manifestation of Preferred Cognitive Style
in Case Studies

Imelda. Imelda, a preferred field sensitive client, talked about her reasons for attempting suicide in a global way: "I was very lonely." She described her adjustment problems in terms of impaired relationships with others: "The people I love just don't seem to understand me the way I am." She asked for direction from the therapist: "Maybe you can tell me how I can get them to understand that I have to be myself."

Harold. Harold, who was preferred field independent, was specific in explaining his reasons for seeking therapy: "I just don't seem to understand what it is that my family and my partners are trying to tell me. It is as if we are speaking different languages, and it is frustrating." He identified what he wanted to get out of therapy with a great deal of self-focus: "I need to regain my self-confidence. I want to feel effective again." Harold made it clear that he wanted the therapist to serve as a consultant to him:

> I've been thinking about my problems, and I think it's a matter of improving my ability to communicate with others. This is where I need your help, because I don't know exactly how to go about this. I do know that I have to work on it myself.

Troy. This client is a preferred field sensitive in all areas except for learning and problem-solving, in which he is bicognitive, and his teaching, supervisory, and counseling styles, in which he is field independent. When asked by the therapist why he thought his parents wanted him to see a therapist, he had a global focus: "They don't like the way I am. They think I'm crazy." Then he went on to describe his adjustment problems as relationship problems with his peers, "My white classmates don't include me in their parties and activities; the black kids at school don't want to have anything to do with me because I'm in the enriched classes and because they think my parents are rich."

Troy then described the mismatch between his field independent teaching style and the learning and problem-solving styles of his African-American peers who are field sensitive: "I've tried to help them out with school, but they say I act superior to them." Troy's preferred field independent learning and problem-solving style was also reflected in his attempts to deal with his problems:

> The one black counselor we have at school gets along with the black kids real well, so I've been watching what he does and I've been trying this myself. Hanging around with my cousin and his fraternity brothers has also helped me. There are times when I feel they almost accept me as one of them.

Wanda. Wanda was fairly well balanced in terms of her development in the field independent and field sensitive styles when she began therapy. Although she is not completely developed in both styles and in all domains of life, she has some initial development in each of the styles in the different personality domains. Her communication style was mostly field independent—her words were well chosen and her messages were short and to-the-point, but she also used nonverbal behaviors when she spoke.

In describing her reasons for seeking therapy, Wanda further demonstrated her style balance; she gave a global description and then proceeded to give details. She said, "The world that I have been putting together for so many years is now falling apart. I see it primarily as a communication problem with my husband and with my children, but I also think that since I've been a manager the way I do things has changed quite a bit."

Her learning and problem-solving style also showed a combination of field sensitivity and field independence:

> I know I have to do most of the work for changing on my own, but I also realize that I am going to need the help of a professional as well. I have been trying to take an objective view of the way I do things, but I'm just too close to the problem to be able to do it on my own.

Wanda's motivation for making changes in her personality was also a mix of the two cognitive styles: "I guess I want to have my cake and eat it too. I do want to be able to be successful and effective in my work so that I can feel good about myself, and I also want to be a good wife and mother so that I will be loved by my husband and children."

Initial Match of Preferred Cognitive Styles

As with cultural styles, the therapist in these case studies attempted to match the cognitive styles of the clients.

Imelda. The therapist matched Imelda's global style by focusing on her feelings: "It must have been terrible to feel so alone." He also focused on her concerns about problems in her relationships with others, indicating that he would be directive in therapy and would serve as a model for her.

Harold. The client's focus on specifics was matched by the therapist's reflection of the specific concerns which Harold had identified as his major problems. The therapist also matched Harold on his self-focus with respect to his reasons for seeking therapy: "Differences in communication style can cause us to feel ineffective and confused." The therapist encouraged Harold to continue being active in therapy and indicated that he would work with Harold in a consultant role. "You've made the right choice in deciding to seek therapy because it can help you improve your communication style and help you to understand the communication styles of others."

Troy. The therapist showed that he was sensitive to Troy's nonverbal communications by reflecting some of the feelings which he saw and heard expressed through Troy's tone of voice, body posture, and mannerisms. The therapist was also sensitive to the fact that Troy's learning style was bicognitive. The therapist recognized that what this client wanted most out of therapy was to have his individuality respected by his mother and to develop a sense of community with his fellow students: "Therapy can help you to relate better to the other kids in school; you can learn things on your own that you can try out with them. In addition, counseling can also help you to get your parents to understand that they have to allow you to be yourself."

Wanda. The therapist matched Wanda's cognitive flex by focusing on both her nonverbal and verbal communication modes. He also used a mix of global and specific features in reflecting what she had said about her problems: "It must be a terrible feeling for you to sense that the world which has given you a lot of security is coming apart. What you would like from therapy is to know how to communicate better and how to avoid conflict with your husband and children." The therapist also addressed her mixed motivational style by saying, "Therapy can help you to feel more effective in your work and also help you to re-establish the closeness you used to have with your family."

Terminating the Initial Session

Following these observations and discussions in the initial session, the therapist uses the final twenty or thirty minutes of the first session to administer instruments to the client in order to help in the assessment of cognitive and cultural styles. These include the Multicultural Experience Inventory (appendix A), Traditionalism-Modernism Inventory (appendix B), the BOLS (appendix D) and the Family Attitudes Scale (appendix L).

While the client is completing the instruments, the therapist examines the notes and ratings made on the Preferred Cultural and Cognitive Styles Observation checklists, comparing these to the self-ratings (see chapter 6) made on the Therapist's Preferred Cognitive and Cultural Styles Instrument made during the course of the session.

Through this exercise the therapist is able to determine how effective he or she is likely to be in matching the client, and makes the decision to either schedule the client for another session, or to make a referral to another therapist. If the therapist is in doubt at this point, it is possible to wait to evaluate the data from the instruments the client has completed before reaching a final decision.

The therapist either schedules the client for another appointment or agrees to call at a later time to give feedback on the initial session, and to inform the client as to whether another appointment should be scheduled or a referral made to another therapist who might be better able to match the client's styles.

SUMMARY

In summary, the first session includes the following techniques and procedures:

- establishment of an atmosphere of nonjudgmental acceptance;
- observation and categorization of client behavior using the Preferred Cultural and Cognitive Styles Observation Checklists;
- matching of client's preferred cultural and cognitive styles;
- therapist's self-assessment of preferred cultural and cognitive therapeutic styles;
- comparison of therapist's and client's preferred styles; and
- scheduling the client for another session, or referral to another therapist or counselor.

SESSION 2

Continuation of Match

The matching strategies which were initiated in the first session are continued in the second. In the initial stages of the second session, the focus of therapy is similar to that of the first session: helping the client to overcome the negative effects of the mismatch syndrome, establishing trust, and continuing to provide a safe atmosphere in which the client can express his or her unique self.

The matching techniques and approaches used by the author in the second session with two of the clients discussed in chapter 1 are presented below.

Imelda. The therapist began the session with Imelda by addressing her by her surname and by making every effort to be warm and supportive. Imelda seemed much happier and more at ease than she had been in the initial session.

To encourage her to feel even more at ease, the therapist asked her about her plans for the spring term. She talked willingly and enthusiastically about her forthcoming games with the basketball team and reported that she was the team captain. She also talked about her plans for attending the state university the following fall.

The therapist's matching behaviors with Imelda included matching both her cultural and cognitive styles, but for clarity of presentation these will be categorized according to five domains of cognitive styles:

1. *Interpersonal relationship style*—the therapist leaned forward in his chair, listening attentively while Imelda talked. He asked questions which allowed her to personalize her accomplishments in sports and in her classes, such as, "You said that you are the captain of your team this year. The other players must think a lot of you" and "You mentioned you had made an A on your term paper for English. What was it about?"

2. *Communication style*—the therapist's facial expressions and tone of voice reflected warmth and support. He maintained eye contact with Imelda while she was talking. The feelings Imelda expressed were reflected through both verbal and nonverbal modes of communication.

3. *Motivational-reward style*—the therapist commented on the fact that Imelda looked happier and seemed more relaxed. He gave verbal and behavioral signs of approval when Imelda talked about her successes. He also showed verbal and nonverbal signs of enthusiasm when Imelda said that she had felt better after the first therapy session.

4. *Problem-solving style*—whenever the opportunity presented itself, the therapist indicated that he would be glad to serve as a model for Imelda. He showed signs of being directive in his style. When Imelda talked about her problems in her relationship with her parents and teachers, he said, "I know that this is hard for you, but we're going to work on your problems together, as a team. You won't feel like you are all alone anymore."

5. *Therapy-teaching-parenting-supervisory style*—in the latter stages of the second session, when the therapist presented the flex theory to Imelda and gave her feedback on his assessments, he personalized the material he presented by relating it to Imelda's interests and life experiences. He used a global-deductive method of presentation; that is, he presented the overall idea or concept first, and then focused on the details, describing how the theory could be applied to her life. For example:

> Value conflicts have been responsible for many of your problems. You and your grandparents used to be very close. When you started getting involved in sports, an activity they felt was not appropriate for girls, they disapproved of you. You felt lonely, rejected, and misunderstood.

Harold. In the case of Harold, the therapist's match behaviors were more oriented towards field independence. Harold entered the office for his second session carrying a portfolio. In it he carried a note pad on which he had analyzed his communication problems with his wife, his children, and his partners. As soon as the session started, he said, "I've been doing some thinking since the last session, and I have made notes on the communication problems I talked about last time. I'd like to read these to you."

1. *Interpersonal relationship style*—the therapist greeted Harold by using his first name, and he allowed Harold to begin the session by reading his notes. As Harold read, the therapist made notes of his own and assumed a formal, business-like manner.

2. *Communication style*—the therapist used an impersonal tone of voice, making minimal use of nonverbal communication. His statements were short and to the point. He chose his words carefully.

3. *Motivational-reward style*—the therapist focused on encouraging self rewards: "It must feel good that you are finally beginning to deal with your problems rather than just worrying about them."

4. *Problem-solving style*—the therapist functioned as a consultant, and made recommendations and suggestions only when Harold asked for help or advice.

5. *Therapy-teaching-parenting-supervisory style*—when the therapist presented the concepts of the flex theory of personality to Harold, he did so by focusing on details and by using a formal-analytic-inductive presentation style: "Communication styles can be classified according to two dimensions: (a) modern-traditional; and (b) field sensitive-field independent.

The Life History

An important aspect of the second session of multicultural therapy is the life history. This technique not only identifies the developmental stages of the client's preferred cultural and cognitive styles, or the unique self, but also reveals how and why the client suppressed his true personality and developed a false self. Specifically, the life history yields the following information:

1. The client's basic foundation for multicultural development: the degree of client motivation to experience diversity and to learn from it, and the degree of openness of the client's learning-experience filters.

2. The number and type of barriers to multicultural development, such as stereotypes (whether negative or positive), ethnocentric behaviors and attitudes, and shyness.

3. The initial manifestations of the unique self in life, and values and belief systems as well as intellectual-occupational interests which may have been suppressed or rejected later on in life.

4. Those periods or phases in the client's life when maximum cultural and cognitive match and mismatch were experienced.

5. The effects of socialization—attitudes of parents toward diversity,

attitudes of other socialization agents and of peers toward diversity, attitudes toward diversity reflected by cultures, communities, and religions in which the client was socialized.

6. The effects of life experiences—how much exposure the client had to diversity over the course of his or her life and the nature and quality of those diversity experiences: the different countries, communities, and neighborhoods in which the client lived; the schools he or she attended; the positive and negative experiences the client had with diversity (e.g., conflicts, experiences with prejudice and rejection).

The life history also provides information which the therapist can use to personalize the third phase of the second session—introducing the client to the flex theory of personality—and to set the goals for multicultural therapy. This life history is an important component of multicultural therapy because it is the initial stage of the process of client empowerment.

Guidelines for Taking the Life History. The therapist introduces the life history by explaining what it is and why it will be useful: "I would like to do a short life history with you in order to better understand how your personality developed and to determine how your adjustment problems started."

A good way to begin a life history is to use what Alfred Adler called the Earliest Childhood Recollection (ECR) (Dreikurs, 1963). The therapist does this by asking the client to recall the earliest memory of childhood. Following the collection of ECRs, the life history is continued by focusing on the following life periods:

Infancy and early childhood. This period would include the childhood years prior to beginning school. Specific questions can be asked in this area:

1. How did you get along with your parents and siblings?
2. Describe the adults that you interacted with.
3. Describe the peers that you played with most often.
4. What jobs or careers were you most interested in?
5. What hobbies did you enjoy?
6. What were your fantasies and daydreams?

Early school experiences and elementary school years. This period involves asking the client about his or her earliest memories of school, and about elementary school experiences. Questions could include:

1. How comfortable did you feel with your first teacher or teachers (counselors, coaches, etc.). With classmates? With the school environment as a whole?
2. What languages did you speak?
3. What classes did you do best in? Which ones were of most interest to you? What awards did you get? What failures did you experience?

4. What countries, regions, states, communities, and neighborhoods did you live in during these early school days?
5. Who were your best friends? What kinds of families did you visit with? Who were your parents' best friends?
6. What jobs or careers were you most interested in?
7. What were your hobbies?
8. When you traveled with your family, where did you go?

Middle school years. The late childhood, early adolescent experiences can be probed with modified versions of those questions used to explore early educational experiences suggested above, as well as by asking the following:

1. Was the middle school you attended different from the elementary school? How so?

High school years. The adolescent years of the client's life history are investigated through the use of the questions suggested above. When necessary, changes are made to make the questions more age-appropriate. Additional questions on job experiences and more in-depth questioning on socializing with peers are included:

1. Did you work during high school? What kind of job did you have? Describe your supervisor(s).
2. Did you date? Describe the background of the people you dated.

Post high school period. Focusing on the period since the client left high school, the therapist asks about:

1. College(s) attended and experiences with professors, courses, reading assignments, peers, and decisions involving career choices;
2. Training program experiences, if any;
3. Military service experience, if appropriate;
4. Marriage and/or meaningful intimate relationships;
5. Jobs or initiation of a career;
6. Travel and other interests; and
7. Religion.

The information collected through the brief life history is invaluable in doing an analysis of match and mismatch experiences and in identifying shifts in cultural and cognitive styles during the client's lifetime.

Imelda's life history, for example, revealed that in her early years she experienced cultural compatibility with her grandparents in terms of their willingness to serve as a support system for her when her mother left home, when her father remarried, and when she experienced conflict with her half sister and stepmother. Later in her life, however, mismatch developed in the area of gender roles when she developed a strong interest in sports.

Harold's early interests in art and music were a good match to his mother's preferred field sensitive cognitive style. She provided Harold with the nurturing he needed because of the rejection he felt from his father and older brother. After his brother's death, Harold shifted to a preferred field independent style in order to please his father.

Introducing the Flex Theory of Personality

Once the life history is completed, the therapist introduces the client to the concept and principles of the flex theory of personality. This third phase of the second session of multicultural therapy reinforces the client empowerment process initiated through the life history. It encourages the client to become an active partner in the therapeutic process. This is done by acquainting the client with the major principles and assumptions of the personality theory on which multicultural therapy is based.

The therapist begins this stage of the session by explaining that multicultural psychotherapy is an approach to personal counseling which is based on the flex theory of personality. The therapist then presents the basic principles of flex theory as follows:

The unique self. Everyone is unique, because every person has a unique arrangement of values, or cultural style, and cognitive style preferences reflected in their personalities.

Cultural styles. There are two kinds of cultural styles, each representing a different set of values and belief systems:

1.   *Traditional style*—typical of rural communities, conservative religions, and of minority and third world cultures. People who are identified with traditional values have a spiritual orientation toward life emphasizing spiritual explanations in explaining the mysteries of life, they are strongly identified with their families and communities of origin, they usually believe in separation of gender and age roles, and they usually believe in strict and autocratic approaches to child rearing.

2.   *Modern style*—typical of urban communities, liberal religions, and of North American and Western European cultures. People who are identified with a modern value system usually emphasize science when explaining the mysteries of life, they have a strong individualistic orientation, they tend to de-emphasize differences in gender and age roles, and they emphasize egalitarianism in child-rearing practices.

Personality styles. There are three kinds of personality styles, each representing different types of cognitive styles:

1. *Field independent style*—people who have a preference for the field independent style tend to be introverted in their orientation to life. They focus on words when communicating with others, and they are usually motivated by material and monetary rewards and by personal achievements. In their thinking and problem-solving styles, people who have a preference for a field independent orientation are more likely to be analytical and inductive, paying a great deal of attention to detail. They usually tend to be nondirective in child-rearing, and in teaching or supervising and counseling others;

2. *Field sensitive style*—people who are preferred field sensitive tend to be extroverted in their general orientation toward life. They tend to focus more on nonverbal than on verbal messages when they are communicating with others. They are usually motivated by the possibility of achieving for others and by social rewards. People with a preferred field sensitive orientation are more global, integrative, and deductive in their thinking and problem-solving styles, and they tend to be very directive in child-rearing and teaching or when they supervise and counsel others; and

3. *Bicognitive style*—people who are bicognitive have the ability to shuttle between the field sensitive and field independent styles. Their choice of style at any particular moment is dependent on the demands of the situation they are in. For example, if the situation demands individual competition they behave in a field independent manner, and if the demand is for cooperation or group competition, they behave in a field sensitive manner. People with a bicognitive orientation can also use elements of both the field sensitive and field independent styles to develop new composite or combination styles. They can evolve communication styles which highlight both verbal and nonverbal behaviors.

Components of styles. Each cognitive and personality style is made up of five components:

- communication style—how people express themselves to others;
- interpersonal relationship style—how people go about establishing relationships with others and how they relate to others;
- motivational style—what people consider rewarding about life;
- learning and problem-solving style—how people learn new things and how they solve problems they are faced with; and
- teaching, parenting, supervisory, and counseling styles—how people impart knowledge or give direction to others, how they guide others and how they provide emotional support.

Personality development. Cultural and cognitive styles are related to personality development. People who are socialized and who have lived in traditional environments (cultures, communities, families, and institutions) are more likely to be preferred field sensitive in cognitive style. Those who are socialized or who have lived in modernistic environments are more likely to be preferred field independent in cognitive style. People who have been socialized in both modern and traditional environments and who have lived in both modern and traditional settings are likely to be bicognitive in their cognitive style.

Variations. Cultural and cognitive styles can vary from being flexible and adaptable to being inflexible and specific to certain environments or situations. People with flexible cultural and cognitive styles have multicultural personalities and are well adjusted to a pluralistic society.

Figures 1–3 which can be found in appendix I may make it easier for the client to follow the therapist's presentation on the important features and concepts of the flex theory of personality. If the client is given copies of Figures 1–3, he or she will be able to refer to them as needed during the course of therapy.

The client should be encouraged to ask questions during the presentation while the therapist attempts to match the style of presentation to the client's preferred learning and problem-solving style. For example, the therapist can personalize the presentation with field sensitive clients by referring to information obtained from the client's life history. On the other hand, with field independent clients, the therapist can focus more on the details of the charts and diagrams and on the specific research which led to the development of the theory (see chapters 2 and 3).

Feedback on Assessment of Preferred Styles

The therapist initiates this phase of the session by referring to the questionnaires the client completed in session one and explaining what their purpose was.

The following is an example of the assessment feedback done with Imelda:

> At the conclusion of the last session I asked you to complete some questionnaires. These were administered to you for the purpose of assessing your preferred cultural and cognitive styles. I have also been doing an assessment during our sessions by noticing your behaviors and by noting what you have said and how you have said it. Let me tell you what my assessments indicate.
> Your preferred cultural style seems to be traditional, but you tend to have modern views in the area of gender role definition.
> Most indicative of your preferred cultural style is the fact that your score on the Traditionalism-Modernism Instrument was +38. You indicated strong agreement on those items which were concerned with family identity, spiritualism, and sense of community, all indications of a traditional orienta-

tion. Despite an overall traditional cultural orientation, you did indicate that you are modern in the domain of gender roles—you believe that men and women should have equal rights.

The therapist continued by giving feedback on the ratings he had made of Imelda's behaviors in the sessions using the Preferred Cultural Styles Observation Instrument showing that her global cultural style was indeed traditional.

In the process of discussing the behavioral ratings he had made, the therapist read excerpts from notes he had made during the course of the therapy sessions to give specific examples which helped to clarify the ratings to the client. (See appendix J for responses given by Imelda to the Traditionalism-Modernism Inventory and for copies of the notes which were made by the therapist as he interacted with Imelda in the initial session.)

Feedback on cognitive style assessment is given in much the same way as it is for cultural style. The following are excerpts from the feedback given to Harold:

> Your preferred cognitive style at the present time is field independent. For example, your score on the Bicognitive Orientation to Life Scale was 31, and you scored in a field independent direction in all five domains. Most revealing of your field independent orientation are the following items: 3, 7, 8, 11, 14, 15, 20, and 21. However, your responses to items 5 and 13 indicate that you also have strong field sensitive interests. My observations of your behaviors during our sessions also show a strong field independent orientation, but again there are some indications that you are somewhat more balanced in the domains of interpersonal relationships and teaching-parenting-supervisory styles.
>
> On a scale of one (no flexibility) to five (maximum flex), your cognitive style balance at the present time appears to be 2.

(See appendix K for the responses given by Harold to the BOLS and for copies of the notes made by the therapist during the first therapy session with Harold.)

The therapist then proceeded to summarize Harold's assessment findings:

> In summary the results of the assessment of your preferred cognitive and cultural styles show that you need to be more flexible in the following domains: cultural; gender roles, time orientation, and child socialization, and cognitive; communication, motivation, and thinking and problem solving.

Establishing the Goals of Therapy

The therapist introduces the final stage of the second session by proposing some tentative goals based on the problems introduced by the client in the first session and on the findings of the assessment. He or she tries to engage the client's help in formulating the goals of therapy. The following example was taken from the case notes on Imelda:

> One goal of therapy can be to help you develop your modernistic cultural style and your field independent cognitive style in order to get your parents, teachers, coaches, and some of your friends at school to understand you better. You could also develop more of your field sensitive and traditional preferred style in order to get your grandparents to understand you better. Would you like to suggest some goals which you would like us to work on?

Imelda answered, "Well, I need to have more friends. Coming to therapy has made me realize that I have been too lonely. I also need to know how to get my teachers and coaches to listen to my ideas." As Imelda spoke, the therapist listed the goals with a marking pencil on a large pad on an easel.

SUMMARY

In summary, the second session included the following techniques and procedures:

- continuation of match
- the life history
- introduction of the concepts of the flex theory of personality
- feedback on assessment of preferred styles
- establishing goals for therapy.

Chapter 8

The Second Stage of Multicultural Therapy and Counseling: Acceptance of the Unique Self and Development of Cultural and Cognitive Flex

In the previous chapter the principal goals of the first session of multicultural therapy and counseling were presented. In this chapter the focus will be on two major objectives: encouraging clients to accept their unique selves, and encouraging them to develop an orientation to life which reflects cultural and cognitive flexibility. Both client and therapist have important roles to play in this phase of multicultural therapy.

SESSIONS 3–5: ENCOURAGING ACCEPTANCE OF THE UNIQUE SELF

The degree of difficulty of this phase of therapy for both clients and therapists can vary depending on the degree to which the clients have suppressed and/or denied their unique selves. The cases of Imelda and Harold are both representative cases. Imelda had continued to develop her preferred style with respect to a modern orientation in gender roles despite pressures to conform from parents and grandparents, but fear of alienating her grandparents and her boyfriend's parents had caused her to downplay her interest in sports and had kept her from establishing close friendships with her coaches and with the other players on her teams. Imelda had not denied her unique self with respect to the other domains of her preferred cultural style and she was fully expressive of her preferred cognitive style. Harold, on the other hand, had undergone a more extensive suppression of both his preferred cultural and cognitive styles. After the death of his brother, he had abandoned his preferred cultural and cognitive styles in order to please his father. Nevertheless, he did occasionally make use of his preferred styles in certain domains of life—his traditionalism and field sensitivity were reflected in the fact that he was the charismatic leader of his company who had established a sense of community for his employees, and in the fact that he was interested in developing an extensive graphic software products line.

The Role of the Client

Clients learn to recognize those pressures to conform to which they have been most vulnerable. They also learn to understand how these pressures are related to the development of the false self and the suppression of the unique self. To identify the sources of pressures to conform, clients have to do thorough and careful assessments of their social environment, including people and institutions.

The sources of pressures to conform can be persons and/or institutions who have played or who are presently playing an important role in the client's life. In the case of Imelda, these included her grandparents, parents, boyfriend's parents, teachers, as well as the traditional community in which she lives. For Harold, sources of pressure to conform include his father, partners, colleagues, and his company.

With the direction of the therapist, clients ask themselves where the conformity pressures are coming from, how these pressures are making themselves felt, how they responded to them in the past, and how they can recognize when they are falling back into using the cultural and cognitive styles of their false selves in response to these pressures.

Still another important task for the client in sessions 3–5 is learning how to come to terms with the discomfort of being different.

The Role of the Therapist or Counselor

In this phase of multicultural therapy, the therapist focuses on establishing an atmosphere which makes it possible for the client to begin exploring and developing the unique self which has been suppressed because of pressures to conform. The therapist facilitates the process of expression and acceptance of the unique self by projecting respect and acceptance of the client's preferred styles, and by giving the client the opportunity to accomplish the matching goals identified in the previous session. These cultural and cognitive match goals have three objectives: a) to help the client to feel comfortable with the unique self, b) to encourage the client to feel pride in that uniqueness, and c) to initiate the process of developing the unique self to its maximum potential.

Examples of the strategies used for achieving match goals were taken from the psychotherapy progress notes and therapeutic plans developed for Imelda and for Harold.

Imelda. The therapist asked Imelda to focus on the first of the cultural match goals established in the previous session: those of developing her modernistic orientation vis-a-vis equality in gender roles, and developing her traditionalistic behaviors in such a way as to encourage her grandparents and parents to understand that her interest in sports is important to her well-being.

The therapist then asked Imelda to think of people in her environment—teachers, coaches, friends of the family, other authority figures, peers, and so forth—who could help her to become more modernistic. After discussing a number of people, Imelda and the therapist settled on one of her basketball coaches, a Hispanic woman, as the best possibility because, according to Imelda's description, this person seemed to have established a good balance in her identification with modern and traditional values.

The therapist encouraged empathy projection by asking the client to answer the following questions: "What is important to your coach? What does she want out of life?" This set the stage for writing a script, based on the coach's preferred cultural and cognitive styles, which Imelda could use when she solicited help from her. While Imelda described what she knew about the coach's interests and personality characteristics, the therapist and Imelda used the concepts from the flex theory of personality to develop hypotheses regarding the coach's preferred cultural and cognitive styles. The therapist then asked Imelda to outline the script she could use for approaching her coach. The therapist and Imelda discussed the script and developed it in order to fit the coach's unique style.

They decided Imelda would begin as follows: "Some time ago you asked me to come to you if I needed any help with my hook shot. Do you have time to help me now?" If the coach were to agree to help Imelda, the script to be used when Imelda and her coach were alone was as follows, "I need your advice on something personal. My parents and grandparents are opposed to my playing on the team. This has been bothering me. Do you have any advice for me?"

The next step in this stage of therapy is role-playing. The therapist assumed the role of the coach while Imelda tried out the script. Following the role-playing exercise, the therapist and Imelda developed a homework assignment which included a day and a time when Imelda would try out the script with her coach. Following this, Imelda was to do ratings and take notes to evaluate the degree of success she felt she had experienced in implementing the script (see appendix F).

If necessary, the therapist and Imelda were to modify the script and either try again with the same person or select someone else identified by Imelda as a possible mentor in her efforts to achieve her cultural styles match goals.

As soon as they felt that the first goal of the cultural match series had been achieved, Imelda and the therapist proceeded to the other goals they had identified. They focused on three life domains: the interpersonal domain; the life activities domain; and the information, media, and travel domain.

In the interpersonal domain, Imelda gained enough confidence through her initial contact with the one Hispanic basketball coach to make a greater effort to get to know both her Hispanic and non-Hispanic coaches better. Most of these coaches proved to be good models for arriving at a comfortable mix of traditional and modern values and belief systems.

From the encouragement she received from her coaches, Imelda made gains in the activities domain—she joined a support group of Hispanic women in sports in one of the local churches in her community. Other changes in the activities domain included going with one of her Hispanic coaches to talk to her grandparents about her commitment to sports. Further, Imelda succeeded in getting her grandparents to go to one of her games. This seemed to improve relations between Imelda and her grandparents, as they became proud of her achievements on the court—they began to view Imelda's accomplishments as achievement for the family.

In the information, media, and travel domain, Imelda started to read books and magazine articles on female athletes such as Nancy Lopez, Babe Zaharias, and some of the tennis players from Spain who had played at Wimbledon. She shared these with her parents and grandparents. Imelda also attended a women's basketball clinic at a state university. At the clinic she met other Hispanic women active in sports who had succeeded in making a good adjustment by combining traditional and modern values.

Harold. For Harold the first goal on the cultural match goals list was to develop traditional values with a view towards improving his relationship with his wife and children.

In the interpersonal domain, the therapist began by asking Harold to think of a script whose objective was to increase his opportunities to interact with his wife. This task appealed to Harold's desire to do things on his own; he immediately began to take notes and to develop a script.

He wrote, "You mentioned some time ago that the Art League is having a reception during an opening at one of the galleries. I would like to go with you if you wouldn't mind." As with Imelda, the therapist discussed the script with Harold, role-played it, and after the necessary modifications, asked Harold to enact it with his wife.

In the activities domain, the therapist and Harold examined some possibilities for activities which could match his traditional cultural style. They decided that Harold could use his interest in photography to strengthen his bond with his wife and children. The family could go on "photography expeditions" together on weekends; they would be able to drive out to a scenic spot or historic town and each family member would take photographs. The family would then talk about what they were trying to accomplish with the composition of the picture, the subject matter, and the lighting.

To develop changes in the information, travel, and media domain, Harold began visiting museums and galleries in neighboring cities and universities in the Bay Area. He began reading magazines and books on photography and art, discovering a special interest in Leonardo da Vinci and others who had combined art with science and mathematics. He and his wife also planned an art tour of Europe for the coming summer, something she had wanted to do for a long time.

Strategies for Meeting Cognitive Style Goals

In addition to establishing and meeting cultural style goals, clients and therapists also strive to meet cognitive style goals in sessions 3–5. These goals also include goals in the interpersonal domain, the activities domain, and the information, travel, and media domain.

Imelda. The therapist and Imelda focused on one of the cognitive styles match goals identified in session 2: the need to further develop Imelda's field sensitive cognitive style in the learning and problem-solving area.

The first step was for Imelda to examine her environment and identify a person who might serve as a model for her. After some discussion, she and the therapist identified one of Imelda's peers, a student described by Imelda as being very successful as a preferred field sensitive student. This time, Imelda was able to develop her script without much help from the therapist. She then role-played the script with the therapist, and together they made some minor changes. Imelda then developed a homework assignment of approaching her friend for help on some of her school work. She carried out the assignment, took notes, and reviewed them at the next session with the therapist.

In the activities domain, Imelda approached the therapist with the suggestion of working as a volunteer in a program available through her church to tutor children in one of the economically depressed neighborhoods in her community. The therapist helped her to see that this could not only help to further develop her field sensitive learning style by her observation of it in others, but it could also help her to develop her field sensitive teaching, counseling, and supervisory style as well.

He suggested that she be observant of those children whose cognitive styles may be preferred field independent as well, because this experience could serve as an early introduction to the next phase of multicultural psychotherapy: mismatch.

Discussion of information, travel, and media experiences which might encourage Imelda to develop her preferred field sensitive style, led to the idea of visiting with her relatives in Mexico. There she was able to visit one of her aunts, a teacher in a Mexican school where field sensitive learning and problem-solving styles are emphasized.

Imelda discussed term papers she was working on with her aunt, who gave Imelda some ideas for using a field sensitive style in her English classes. She also lent Imelda some of the texts and workbooks which are used in grammar and literature classes in Mexico. Imelda and the therapist reviewed these and identified materials which could be helpful in Imelda's development.

Harold. The cognitive style goal upon which Harold decided to focus was communication style. The therapist and he agreed that Harold would develop his field sensitive communication style in order to better match those of his wife and children, and also in order to further develop that preferred style which he had abandoned after his brother's death.

Within the interpersonal domain, the therapist encouraged Harold to review his social environment and identify the best field sensitive communicator he had ever known. Harold recalled a professor at his alma mater who was very developed in terms of field sensitive communication style. When Harold was a student, it was this professor who had encouraged him to take up photography as a hobby. Harold developed a script for approaching the professor, and after trying the script out with the therapist, some minor changes were made. Harold then made plans for implementing the script and for evaluating its effectiveness.

In an effort to match his field sensitive style within the activities domain, Harold enrolled in advanced photography classes at one of the community colleges near his home.

In the information, travel, and media domain, Harold and his wife went on a European tour which included seminars in art and photography. Both the content and the teaching style of classes as described in the travel brochures seemed to be predominantly field sensitive in orientation.

Conformity Pressures and the Adoption of a False Self

Recognizing and overcoming pressures to conform are examined in sessions 4 and 5. There are three components to this phase of client empowerment:

- becoming aware of conformity pressures both with respect to the source and the type of pressure;
- becoming aware of the mismatch situations most associated with conformity pressures; and
- avoiding self-criticism and other types of negative thinking which could result in falling back into the styles of the false self.

Imelda and the therapist discussed those people and institutions that were the greatest source of pressures to conform. They identified her parents, her grandparents, her boyfriend, and her school. Her parents, grandparents, and boyfriend were the greatest source of conformity pressures for cultural styles. Her school, on the other hand, and more specifically her English teacher, were the greatest source of this type of pressure with respect to cognitive styles.

The therapist and Imelda discussed how these pressures were applied to her and how she experienced them. The focus here was on the negative thinking triggered by these pressures: "I tell myself I'm being too different, too rebellious, that I'm not obedient, that I'm bad."

An analysis of the sources of pressures to conform for Harold identified his father, his partners, and the professional societies to which he belonged. Harold discovered that he experienced this pressure as guilt:

> I feel like I'm letting my partners down; I feel that I cannot be the kind of son my father always wanted, especially since my brother passed away. When I am with my colleagues at professional meetings, I feel that I don't really belong with them, with their interests and ways of doing things—I feel like a misfit.

With the help of the therapist Imelda became aware of mismatch situations in her daily life. She came to recognize that on the days that she was playing in a game, her parents and grandparents applied the strongest pressure to have her conform to the traditional cultural style. This usually led to heated arguments, upsetting Imelda, and affecting her concentration in the game. It was at these times, she realized, that she was most vulnerable to falling back into the styles of her false self.

For Harold the strongest instances of pressures to conform were when he visited his father, or when he talked to him on the phone, and especially when Harold talked to his father about business, or about his new ideas for product development. They got along well when they discussed other topics such as politics or sports.

With his partners Harold recognized that the strongest pressures to conform, especially with respect to cognitive styles, were exerted when he made a presentation about his ideas for new product development, or when he discussed personnel problems with them.

In the area of avoiding self-blame, self-criticism, and other forms of negative thinking, the therapist worked with both Imelda and Harold to get them to recognize their tendencies towards these forms of thinking. These cognitive distortions, identified by Ellis (1970) and by Beck (1976) in their work with neurotic and depressed clients, often trigger a return to the cognitive style of the false self.

Enhancing Self-Esteem

A necessary accompaniment to the strategies for empowerment is the development of clients' self-esteem and sense of mastery. The therapist not only assists clients in facilitating self-discovery, but also helps clients recognize that they should be proud of their unique selves. Further, the therapist helps clients to recognize and enjoy the rewards which result from match experiences. Finally, the therapist assists clients in realizing the positive aspects of feeling that they are gaining control over their own destiny.

Self-acceptance. For Imelda, growth in self-acceptance and pride was expressed in the feeling that she did not have to be as dependent on others for support as she had been in the past: "I feel that I can rely on myself more now. I like myself more, and I don't feel that I need others to approve of me as much anymore."

Harold's growing pride in his unique self and his self-acceptance were reflected in his feelings of enthusiasm about his work. "I feel excited about my work and my ideas again. I feel creative for the first time in a long time."

Mastery. For Imelda, gaining more control over her life, and feeling less like a victim of circumstances was a result of knowing what to anticipate. Her feeling that she could deal with situations more effectively without getting upset and angry added to this realization of mastery:

> I know what's coming now, and I feel more prepared for it. I don't lose my temper as much as I used to because I no longer feel like I have to convince people; I just tell them how I feel and then take it as it is. There are no longer the big conflicts I had with my parents and grandparents.

For Harold mastery was equated with the loss of the feeling of disorientation and confusion: "I feel at peace with myself. I feel I understand myself and others better."

SUMMARY

In summary, sessions 3, 4, and 5 included the following techniques and procedures:

- selection of a cultural match goal from the list developed in the second session;
- identification of a model;
- empathy projection vis-a-vis the model;
- identification of the model's preferred styles;
- developing a script for approaching the model;
- role-playing;
- homework assignment: enacting the script;
- evaluation of homework; and
- modification of script and re-enactment (if necessary).

These procedures and techniques are also used for achieving cognitive match goals:

- awareness of sources of conformity pressures;
- identification of mismatch situations associated with conformity pressures;
- avoidance of self-criticism and cognitive distortions; and
- development of feelings of self-acceptance and mastery.

SESSIONS 6-10: ENCOURAGING CULTURAL AND COGNITIVE FLEX

In this phase of therapy the therapist or counselor helps the client to develop unfamiliar, or non-preferred cultural and cognitive styles in order to initiate the process of multicultural personality development. The therapist also encourages the development of client mastery and empowerment.

Some clients have used various aspects of these unfamiliar or less preferred styles in their efforts to conform (i.e., in their false selves) in the face of pressures to conform. For example, Imelda tried to force herself to be field independent in her cognitive style even though she was preferred field sensitive. She did this because she felt pressured to behave like most of her classmates. Harold, on the other hand, tried to adopt a modernistic orientation in his relationships with his wife and children in his effort to be more like his father.

This phase of therapy involves the use of mismatch. Mismatch is introduced to the client gradually, in the context of match, and only after the client feels comfortable with his or her unique self.

As therapists introduce clients to mismatch, they continue to match clients' preferred cognitive and cultural styles in order to encourage the continued development of the preferred styles while the unfamiliar styles are being developed.

Distribution of the Sessions. As discussed in the match phase of therapy, the therapist makes a decision about the number of sessions necessary for achieving the client's mismatch goals, based on the number of goals to be achieved and the client's rate of progress. Some clients require more time, and others less. Since successful accomplishment of homework tasks is a crucial part of this phase of therapy, the number of sessions needed will depend on the difficulty of achieving the goals, the motivation of the client, and the rapidity with which the techniques of the Multicultural Model can be learned.

Introducing Mismatch

Mismatch is introduced only after the client has overcome most of the negative symptoms of the mismatch syndrome. The client should feel comfortable and self-confident, and feelings of alienation, anger, anxiety, and defensiveness should have subsided before mismatch is introduced.

The therapist should withhold the introduction of mismatch processes until the client begins to feel some pride in the unique self and some sense of mastery over his or her own destiny. Mismatch should always be introduced gradually and with caution, to avoid re-emergence of the symptoms of the mismatch syndrome.

The processes and techniques of therapy used to achieve mismatch goals are similar to those used to achieve match goals: there is an examination of the client's social environment for the purpose of identifying persons and institutions which the client should learn to match. Again, as with match, techniques include empathy projection, script writing, role-playing, homework assignments to try out scripts, assessment, and if necessary, reworking of the script and trying again.

In addition to the step-by-step process summarized above, the procedures for achieving mismatch goals introduces two new therapeutic techniques: awareness of feelings and diversity challenges.

Awareness of feelings is an introspective technique requiring the clients to recognize their feelings at a given moment in time. Clients ask themselves, "How am I feeling right now?" "Is this the right time for me to attempt match?"

Awareness of feelings is important when clients are trying to match people or institutions with whom they have experienced conflicts in the past.

Diversity challenges are similar to the emersion approach used for teaching languages: the person is placed in a situation in which only the new language is spoken in order to facilitate learning. In multicultural psychotherapy, clients are encouraged to interact with persons or to adapt to sociocultural environments that can stimulate development of the new values and personality characteristics they will need in order to achieve flex. Diversity challenges require the person to adopt new styles promoting the development of flex.

Imelda. One of Imelda's mismatch goals was to adopt modernistic values and belief systems in domains other than equality in gender roles. Achieving this goal would make it possible for her to develop a wider and more diverse circle of friends.

The process followed in achieving Imelda's first mismatch goal included the therapist's review of the definitions of modern values and belief systems, as well as examples he had presented to her when he introduced the flex theory of personality in the second session (see Chapter 7):

> When we discussed values in our second session, I said that modern values are typical of people who live in large cities. They are also typical of those who tend to be members of liberal Protestant religions and whose lives are relatively free of the pressures of tradition and family. People with modern values tend be very individualistic in their orientations to life. Some examples of modern values that I presented at that time included individual competition and achievement, and independence from the family. Do you think you would be okay trying values like these?

With this question the therapist gave Imelda the opportunity to express any reservations she might have about trying out behaviors reflecting modern values. These reservations could have taken two forms: feeling uncomfortable using nonpreferred styles because these are associated with pressures to conform or feelings of discomfort because these are associated with others, or with institutions with which the client has had negative experiences in the past.

For example, Imelda said that she had some trouble accepting modern values because these were associated with the pressures to conform she had experienced from her father and stepmother. She also reported that modern values made her uncomfortable because she associated these with the parents of an Anglo boy she had once dated and who she felt had rejected her because she was Hispanic.

At the same time, Imelda said, "You know I feel as if I'm already learning to use modern values, because I am spending more time with my coaches. Getting closer to the Anglo coaches has also helped me to realize that not all Anglos are the same." The therapist reinforced her for this insight.

The therapist and Imelda reviewed her social environment in order to identify people and institutions that could help her to achieve her mismatch goals. Also examined were the notes from her life history. The search led to the identification of Betty, one of her Anglo teammates on the basketball team, who was very individually competitive, and who seemed financially and emotionally independent of her family.

The third step in developing mismatch goals for Imelda was empathy projection. She and the therapist discussed Betty:

Therapist: What do you think Betty wants out of life?

Imelda: Well, I think she wants to be the best player on the team, because she likes to have her name mentioned in assemblies when we win games. There have been times when I have disliked her because of the way she is—so competitive and all, but she has been friendly to me. She has invited me to parties at her house and at her friends' houses.

Awareness of feelings is yet another technique the therapist used with Imelda in encouraging her to adopt modernistic values:

Therapist: How do you feel right now?

Imelda: I don't feel so good; I'm upset because my Dad and I got into a big argument about my half sister again last night.

Therapist: So this would not be a good time for you to try to match someone like Betty. You need to try it when you're feeling better about things.

Imelda: Yes, I see. That makes sense. Otherwise I'm likely to botch it up, right?

Imelda and the therapist discussed the possible script Imelda could use in approaching her teammate for help. Recognizing that Imelda was field sensitive in terms of learning and problem-solving style, the therapist modeled for her and worked cooperatively with her in developing the script. Using a large pad on an easel, the therapist began by making suggestions and then encouraged Imelda to come up with ideas. As the process continued, Imelda did most of the work on her own.

After Imelda was satisfied with her script, she and the therapist role-played it, making changes suggested as the roles were tested. Imelda decided when and where to actually try the script with Betty: she decided to approach her during the next practice session and ask her if she could walk home with her since they lived near each other.

Immediately after trying out the script with Betty, Imelda evaluated its effectiveness.

A second mismatch goal that Imelda and the therapist identified was to learn to communicate in a field independent style. They felt that this style would be more effective in matching the preferred style of her English teacher, and that if match were successful it might make the teacher more receptive to becoming more flexible in her teaching style. The process for achieving this goal included the therapist's reviewing the definition and examples of the field independent cognitive style with a focus on communication styles:

Therapist: When we talked about cognitive styles, I said that field independent styles were usually the preferred styles of people who are modern in their cultural style. We talked about how preferred field independent people communicate with others in messages which are short and to-the-point. These people usually do not include any personal information or feelings in what they say.

Imelda: Yes, that describes my English teacher.

Therapist: Do you think it would be hard for you to communicate in a field independent style?

Imelda: I can do it, but I have a negative reaction to it because that's the way my parents talk to me when they are angry with me. Besides, I don't think I have been able to ever get along with teachers who talk that way. Lately, though, I have noticed that some of my coaches talk that way and I do like them, so I guess it's okay.

As Imelda recognized that some of her coaches used the field independent style to communicate, she identified one of them as the person she could try her script with once it was developed.

The therapist led Imelda in empathy projection:

Therapist: What do you think your English teacher wants out of life?

Imelda: I think she wants to be voted the best teacher so that she can get the annual teaching award.

Therapist: How do you think she is feeling these days?

Imelda: She was one of three teachers nominated for the award, so I think she feels pretty good right now.

Again, the therapist reminds Imelda to monitor her own feelings and to choose a time to try her script when she is not angry or upset.

Imelda and the therapist discussed a possible script, wrote one, and role-played it, making changes as they saw necessary. Imelda tried out the script, evaluated it, and modified it. After trial and evaluation the therapist and client reworked it as necessary until they were satisfied with it.

Concurrently with script writing and homework assignments for achieving mismatch goals, Imelda, with the help of the therapist, was also identifying diversity challenges that she would try:

1. She would go to a party at which she was likely to be the only

Hispanic in attendance. Imelda had turned down Betty's earlier invitations since she had been uncomfortable with the thought of being the only Hispanic in the group. Accepting an invitation now would be a good immersion opportunity for learning how to use modernistic values in interpersonal relationships.

   2.   Imelda decided to participate in teacher-student get-acquainted sessions sponsored by the student council. This experience would give Imelda an opportunity to interact with teachers who were field independent in communication style. It would also provide an opportunity to try out the field independent communication behaviors she was learning through script writing and role-playing with the therapist.

   Throughout this phase of therapy, the therapist gave Imelda social rewards as she progressed. He gave frequent encouragement by saying, "I'm very proud of the progress you are making."

   Realizing Imelda's preferred styles, the therapist used modeling as a teaching style in developing the scripts and in role-playing them while Imelda watched; saying, for example, "Here is the way I would do it," and then demonstrating what he would say and do in communicating with someone who was preferred field independent.

SUMMARY

   In summary, sessions 6–10 focused on the introduction of mismatch using the following techniques and procedures:

- review of the characteristics of unfamiliar cultural and cognitive styles;
- allowing the client to express feelings about these values and styles;
- review of the client's social environment and of life history interview notes in order to identify people and institutions that can help the client to achieve mismatch goals;
- empathy projection;
- awareness of feelings;
- script writing and role-playing; and
- script enactment and evaluation.

Chapter 9

Assessment of Progress in Flex Development

Once the mismatch phase of Multicultural Psychotherapy is well underway, the therapist should assess the client again in order to obtain a systematic view of the degree of client progress in the various areas and domains of cultural and cognitive styles. The information obtained by the therapist then can be compared with the data obtained from the earlier assessment. The comparison helps the therapist to determine if there is any need to make changes in the therapeutic plan. This assessment should answer two principal questions: How many and which of the goals have been met? Which domains or areas of cultural and cognitive styles will require additional work?

For most clients this re-assessment can be done in session 11 or 12, but this can vary depending on the degree of progress made by the client. The therapist is the best judge of when it is best to assess progress. Feedback to the client should be done during the session following an assessment.

The assessment phase of Multicultural Therapy also requires that the therapist do a self-evaluation. This evaluation will focus on whether or not the therapist is matching and mismatching the client effectively; on whether to give additional emphasis to certain strategies or to certain domains of cultural and cognitive styles; and on whether the therapist's cultural and cognitive style preferences are in any way interfering with the development of client flex.

Client and therapist assessment is multimodal. It involves the use of personality and value inventories, behavioral (verbal and nonverbal) ratings, and the evaluation of the degree of progress made in homework assignments. This chapter will review both the assessment procedures for clients and therapists, as well as feedback procedures used with the client after the assessment results have been evaluated.

91

ASSESSING CLIENT PROGRESS

The therapist introduces the assessment of progress phase of therapy to the client by emphasizing the need to review the degree of progress being made in the therapeutic plan that was established in the second or third session. The therapist then re-administers the instruments used in the initial session.

To evaluate cultural style the therapist again uses the Traditionalism-Modernism Inventory, the Cultural Styles Observation Check-list, and the Multicultural Experience Inventory. In addition to these instruments, the therapist examines the progress made in homework assignments and diversity challenges. Still another indicator of progress in multicultural therapy is the development of more positive attitudes towards people and groups whom the client considers to be different from him or herself.

After re-administering the Traditionalism-Modernism Inventory, the therapist focuses on each of the three scores: the total traditionalism score, the total modernism score, and the traditionalism-modernism balance score.

The total traditionalism and the total modernism scores are compared to the scores obtained after the first administration of the instrument. The change score is considered in light of the client's goals with respect to the need to be more traditional or more modern in cultural style. The traditionalism-modernism balance score is a crucial indicator of progress towards the development of cultural flex, because it is arrived at by adding the total traditionalism score and the total modernism score. The balance score is compared to the balance score obtained after the first administration of the inventory.

Ratings made by the therapist on the cultural styles observation check-list in the session prior to the assessment session are compared to those made in the first session. The main areas of focus are:

- behaviors (verbal and nonverbal) associated with traditional values;
- behaviors (verbal and nonverbal) associated with modern values;
- the degree of balance between traditional and modern behaviors; and
- the behaviors which are reflective of a combination of traditional and modern values.

Beyond re-administering the instruments, the therapist also takes into account progress on homework assignments when assessing progress. One gage of success on the homework assignments is the ratings and notes made by the client upon completion of implementation of scripts.

The degree of progress made in diversity challenges is also useful in assessing overall progress. At this time, the therapist evaluates the number of challenges taken and the degree of success (as judged by the client) achieved on each diversity challenge.

The therapist directs the client to complete the Multicultural Experience Inventory again. The total score is compared to that obtained in the previous administration. Comparison of scores on individual items, such as being involved in more activities with people of other ethnic groups, is also important.

The total score on the Multiculturalism Experience Inventory may be more important as an indicator of progress for some clients than it is for others. With respect to the four case studies examined in this book, the total score was more important to Imelda, Wanda, and Troy than it was to Harold. For Harold, the more important goal of multiculturalism, at least at that point in time, involved being more flexible with respect to cultural and cognitive styles within his own cultural group, while it was less important for him to relate more effectively to members of other sociocultural groups.

Finally, an evaluation of the client's progress on attitudes towards the different is important in assessing the development of cultural flex. The therapist notes the degree of motivation and enthusiasm exhibited by the client when executing homework assignments and diversity challenges. The therapist also considers comments the client has made in therapy about people and groups which the client considers to be different from him or herself.

Progress made by the client on the cognitive styles goals is also assessed by re-administering instruments given in the initial session. The therapist then compares the total field independence score and the total field sensitive score to those achieved in the first administration. The latter scores are examined in light of the client's therapeutic goals with respect to the need to be more field independent or field sensitive in cognitive style. The balance score is also compared to the earlier balance score and examined in view of the development of cognitive flex.

Ratings on the Preferred Cognitive Styles Observation Check-list made during sessions 1 and 2 are compared with ratings made in the sessions prior to the assessment session. The therapist evaluates specific domains of cognitive style such as communication, learning and problem-solving, and so forth. He or she rates behaviors, both verbal and nonverbal, associated with field sensitivity and with field independence. Using the check-list, the therapist also examines the degree of balance between field independent and field sensitive behaviors as well as the development of behaviors which are a combination of the two cognitive styles.

As with the assessment of the development of cultural flex, the therapist reviews progress on homework assignments, on diversity challenges, and on clients' change in attitudes and stereotypes regarding people and groups different from themselves.

FEEDBACK TO THE CLIENT

Before giving any feedback, the therapist must ensure that a good rapport has been established with the client. In all cases the positive feedback should be given before any barriers to growth are discussed.

With preferred field sensitive and traditional clients such as Imelda, the therapist is advised to start with the global picture and then proceed to specifics, and to use personal examples from therapy notes to personalize the feedback as much as possible. For the preferred field independent and modern client such as Harold, however, the therapist should start with details and work up to the global, emphasizing concepts rather than personalizing communications.

The client must be encouraged to understand the importance of his or her active participation in those situations in which it is necessary to change the therapeutic plan and/or in developing strategies for goals which have not yet been achieved.

Excerpts from the feedback given to two of the case study clients, Imelda and Harold, illustrate the procedures and strategies implemented to modify the therapeutic plan and/or to work more effectively on those goals where little or no progress has been made. Note that the feedback is individualized to match the unique personality style of each client; in the examples given below, efforts to match are set off by italics in parentheses. Imelda's preferred cultural and cognitive styles are traditional and field sensitive respectively. Therefore, the therapist is directive in his approach and he personalizes feedback. He also emphasizes social rewards and improvement of sense of community with respect to therapy goals achieved.

Imelda

Therapist: The assessment I have done shows that you have made excellent progress in developing modern cultural styles. You've also made good progress in developing the field independent cognitive style. You have continued to develop in the traditional cultural style and in the field sensitive cognitive style as well. You seem to be getting along better with others—your parents, your grandparents, teachers, coaches, and friends. I'm very proud of your progress *(personalizing and giving social rewards).*

   The results of the Traditionalism-Modernism Inventory show that your modernism score is now 42 whereas it was 38 when you first took the inventory about ten weeks ago. What impresses me most is your balance score, or flex score; when you first took the Traditionalism-Modernism Inventory, your score was lopsided in the direction of traditionalism, but this time your score indicated that you are more balanced in your cultural styles.

On the ratings I have made in our sessions, I noticed that you are tending to use both traditional and modern behaviors; in the first few sessions, most of your behaviors were traditional.

I'm also impressed by how well you've done on your homework assignments and on diversity challenges. I looked though the ratings you made after your homework and diversity challenges; they indicate that you were very successful in what you did.

Your attitude towards Anglo peers and teachers at your school has also improved a great deal. You started out making angry and negative comments about Anglos in the first few sessions, but these have been replaced by more positive statements in the last four sessions. The results of the Multiculturalism Experience Inventory also show that you are now doing more things with Anglo friends and with your Anglo coaches and teachers.

The results of the assessment show that you have made good progress in learning how to use field independent cognitive styles. The results of the Bicognitive Orientation to Life Scale show that your field independent score has changed from 12 to 32. At the same time your field sensitive score and bicognitive flex, or balance scores, have also improved.

The ratings on the Preferred Cognitive Styles Observation Check-list show that the two domains in which you still need to make progress is in field independent learning and problem-solving; and teaching, counseling, and supervisory styles. The homework assignment and diversity challenge ratings you made show that you are still uncomfortable in these two domains.

These are the two areas, or domains, we need to concentrate on in the next few sessions. Here is what I would suggest: Let's do some scripts together which will concentrate on using some of the field independent behaviors and strategies in learning and problem-solving; and teaching, counseling, and supervisory styles.

I will play roles in which I will use field independent learning/problem-solving or teaching-counseling-supervisory styles, and you will match my behaviors and strategies.

I would also suggest that you do more diversity challenges in which you have to use field independent styles for learning and teaching. Here is one suggestion: volunteer to assist some of your coaches who use field independent approaches to coaching when they work with the junior varsity team.

Harold's preferred styles are modern and field independent, so the therapist's style for giving feedback is data-centered, much like that of a scientist reporting research findings. He also encourages the client to participate actively in the session. Improvement in therapy focuses on increased self-efficacy and individual achievement.

Harold

The therapist prepared some bar graphs on a large tablet resting on an easel.

Therapist: These charts which I prepared *(to match Harold's field independent preferred learning style)* show the degree of progress you have made *(emphasis on modernistic style of individual achievement)* between the first administration of the instruments and those done more recently. As you can see, you have made great progress in all of the domains of the traditional cultural styles. You made a higher traditionalism score on the Traditionalism-Modernism Inventory, and the ratings made on the Preferred Cultural Styles Observation Check-list show growth in all areas, particularly in communication.

You also have been expressing more positive attitudes toward traditionally oriented people in your most recent sessions. Your self-ratings on homework and diversity challenge assignments are quite good.

However, there is one area in which you still need to make progress — you still look somewhat uncomfortable when you interact with traditionally oriented people, and you still have a tendency to interrupt them while they are talking. You need to work on these areas *(emphasis on individual effort)*. These same problems show up in the communication domain of the cognitive styles chart.

My ratings, as well as yours on homework and diversity challenge assignments, show that your messages still tend to be too short and that you are not very self-disclosing when you converse with others. Here are some of the evaluation feedback sheets you completed after doing your homework assignments and diversity challenges. As you can see they show that you often rate yourself as being too abrupt and self-conscious; you often behaved as if you were in too much of a hurry to complete the assignment.

I have some suggestions for improvements in this area. I would like your input on these *(independent orientation of the modernistic-field independent preferred client)*. I would like for you to try writing some more scripts that focus on a traditional communication style and use of traditional behaviors in communication. For some ideas I'd like you to read the communication chapter in Aaron Beck's book, *Love Is Never Enough* (1988). I would also suggest role playing in which I use field sensitive and traditional communication behaviors, and you attempt to match me.

A few sessions back you showed me some literature on marriage encounter weekend workshops for couples sponsored by your church. I remember that some of the exercises described in the brochure were oriented towards the traditional cultural style—writing letters to spouses and open discussions of feelings in small groups. I think that this experience would help to develop your field sensitive and traditional modes of communication and of interacting with others.

ASSESSING THE THERAPIST

The assessment phase of Multicultural Psychotherapy focuses on the therapist as well as on the client. Ratings of cultural and cognitive therapeutic styles made in sessions 1 and 2 are compared with those made in the two sessions prior to the assessment session. The questions on which assessment of the therapist is focused are as follows: How effectively is the therapist matching and mismatching the client? Is the client's false self or preferred style negatively affecting the therapist's ability to flex in therapy and achieve the goals of the therapeutic plan?

For example, while he was doing therapy with Imelda and Harold, the therapist discovered that the clients' dominant styles had a "pull" effect in the mismatch phase of therapy. With Imelda, the therapist tended to start the sessions of the mismatch phase in a modern mode, but Imelda's strong traditional orientation resulted in "pulling" the therapist to match her.

With Harold, on the other hand, the "pull" was in the direction of field independent therapeutic behaviors, especially in the domain of communication and interpersonal relationship styles. In this case, the therapist started the sessions of the mismatch phase in a field sensitive mode, but after a few minutes found himself shifting to field independent behaviors to match Harold's style. These findings gave the therapist valuable insight into his own preferred styles and how he was failing to encourage the development of client flex.

The therapist took a number of steps to address his concerns: (a) consulting with a colleague to discuss possible countertransference issues with Imelda and Harold; (b) the therapist remained cognizant of those client behaviors (both verbal and nonverbal), that elicited the "triggering" or "pull" effects, using these as warning signs in his attempt to prevent the tendency to be pulled into match behaviors; (c) he called these problems to the attention of the clients so that they could assist in the therapist's attempt to resist "pull" by recognizing and discussing it with him when it happened; and (d) the therapist developed script-writing exercises, and role-played the scripts using a modified version of the empty chair technique (Levitsky & Perls, 1970), in front of a video camera. The therapist played the roles of both client and therapist moving from one chair to the other and in this way tried out response strategies to client behaviors which had a "pull" effect on therapeutic style. He then watched the videotape, and rated his therapeutic behaviors, using the two observation checklists.

SUMMARY

In summary, the assessment and feedback sessions included the following techniques and procedures:

- making a decision as to the session in which it is most appropriate to assess progress;
- preparing the client for re-administration of the instruments used in the first session;
- re-administering the instruments;
- scoring and comparing new scores to those obtained previously, comparing ratings on the Preferred Cognitive and Cultural Styles Observation checklists, evaluating progress on homework assignments, diversity challenges, and in the development of positive attitudes toward the "different";
- giving feedback to the client;
- making changes in the therapeutic plan, making additional assignments to client, if necessary;
- therapist self-assessment; and
- eliminating therapist behaviors which interfere with the development of client flex.

Chapter 10

The Client as Change Agent and Multicultural Ambassador

The principal goal of the fourth and final phase of multicultural psychotherapy is to complete the task of client empowerment. The specific objective of this stage of therapy is to encourage the client to become an active participant in the development of a multicultural society.

FINAL PHASE OF THERAPY

This final phase of therapy addresses an issue of major concern to the "different"—the fear that psychotherapy will be used as a tool to encourage client conformity and assimilation to the values and life styles of the power structure. The African-Martiniquean psychiatrist Franz Fanon (see Bulhan, 1985) exposed this colonialist perspective in traditional psychoanalytic personality theories and therapies. Bulhan (1985), in his book *Franz Fanon and the Psychology of Oppression,* writes:

> How can an intervention liberate the patient from social oppression when the 'therapist-patient' relationship itself is suffused with the inequities, non-reciprocity, elitism, and sadomasochism of the oppressive social order? Can there be realistic grounds for changing self-defeating behaviors and a negative self-concept in a context in which only the 'doctor' initiates and the 'patient' accommodates, where one is powerful and the other powerless? (p. 272)

Ryan (1971) has also criticized the "blame the victim" orientation of many of the traditional personality theories and psychotherapies. The client-as-activist phase of multicultural therapy, then, represents a radical departure from traditional forms of psychotherapy and counseling.

Role of Client

There are four roles which the client is encouraged to play:

1. *The role of change agent.* In this role the client helps to create changes in the institutions and agencies which have had a significant impact on him or her. For Imelda and Troy, the focus of change was on the schools they attend, while for Wanda and Harold, it was on their work places.

2. *The role of educator.* In this capacity the client introduces people who have the power to influence the policies and practices of institutions and agencies to the concepts of the flex theory of personality and to the Multicultural Model of Psychotherapy. The objective is to encourage "power holders" to better understand and to attempt to resolve problems of mismatch.

3. *The role of peer counselor.* The client provides emotional support and facilitates change and empowerment in those of his peers who are victims of mismatch shock.

4. *The role of multicultural ambassador.* As an ambassador the client promotes the development of multicultural environments which encourage understanding and cooperation among different peoples and groups.

As the therapist encourages clients to learn concepts, techniques and procedures by which they can change the environment and influence others, he or she also warns against the use of what is learned for the purpose of manipulating others. The therapist points out that the knowledge possessed by the client is potentially damaging, and must be used in responsible ways. The client is encouraged to keep the principal goal of environmental change in mind, and to help make society sensitive to the cultural and individual differences of all its citizens.

Wanda as Change Agent. As Wanda talked about her conflicts with her husband and children, she arrived at the insight that a major problem for both herself and for her colleagues had to do with the fact that the worlds of career and of family are too separated in day-to-day life. She reported, for example, that in conversations she had with her colleagues she had learned that several of them were having problems in their marriages; she also found that they too had guilt feelings because they were not able to spend more time with family members.

During coffee breaks and over lunch Wanda's colleagues often talked of how their wives and children complained that they were spending too much time at the office or doing too much company work at home. With the guidance of the therapist, Wanda concluded that if she made use of the concepts of the flex theory and of the Multicultural Model, she might be able to affect changes which could close the gap between the worlds of career and of family for her colleagues and for herself.

Wanda's goal was to encourage her colleagues on the management team to become more family-centered through company-sponsored social events. In this way, the families could be helped to understand the work the management team was doing and to feel that they were a part of these efforts.

The therapist helped Wanda toward reaching this goal. He asked her to identify one or more colleagues who might be able to assist her. After some thought she settled on Harry, her closest friend on the management team. They had both discussed this problem, and had concluded that it was affecting their home lives as well as their work. Wanda felt that if she approached Harry for help on this "project," he would be willing to cooperate.

The therapist asked Wanda to try to put herself in her colleagues' shoes and think about what it was that they might want out of life. Wanda ventured:

> I think our goals are all pretty much the same; that is, we all want to be CEOs, or at least VPs, at some point. I also think that we want to do it without sacrificing our families in the process. I've been reading *Habits of the Heart* [by Bellah et al.], and that first chapter about the guy who eventually loses his wife and kids because he was spending too much time promoting his career really hit home.

The therapist then asked Wanda to think of a way in which she and the members of her management team could achieve the goal of closing the gap between the worlds of career and of family. After some discussion, Wanda arrived at the idea of proposing a day-long company social activity during a weekend. This activity would allow families of the members of the management team to participate in planned tours of the plant, play games, have meals together, and watch video presentations aimed at acquainting family members with the type of work done by the company and the management team. The activities would be planned to be both informative and fun.

Wanda and the therapist discussed writing a script for making the presentation to Harry, Wanda's friend and potential ally. They also outlined another script for presenting the idea at one of the management team meetings.

Wanda decided that she would prepare the scripts on her own and then bring them to the next therapy session where she and the therapist would discuss them and then do role-playing with them.

As homework, Wanda decided that she would approach Harry with her idea during a coffee break. At the same time she would share with him the script for introducing the activity to the management team. She would incorporate Harry's suggestions for changes, and ask him for input as to the best time to present the idea. In asking Harry to make these decisions, Wanda practiced the empathy projection and feeling awareness exercises that she had used in the mismatch phase of therapy.

After meeting with Harry, Wanda made some changes in the script which he had suggested. She then role-played the modified script with the therapist and made additional changes as necessary. She then made plans for enacting the script with Harry's help. The script was implemented and an evaluation of script effectiveness was done. The results of the evaluation were discussed with the therapist.

In summary, encouraging the client to assume the role of change agent included the following techniques and procedures:

- identification of institutional change goal
- identification of an ally
- empathy projection
- development of preliminary plan to discuss with ally
- script writing to enlist ally's support and to achieve goal (either prepared by client independently or in collaboration with the therapist depending on goals of therapy plan)
- ally is approached for suggestions in changes in plan and/or script.

Imelda as Change Agent. Gender roles are usually separated in traditional societies, resulting in pressures to conform for women athletes, since athletics are usually seen as the exclusive domain of men. Imelda faced this problem.

Having experienced the disapproval of parents, grandparents, and other authority figures in her traditional community, and having realized that other players and coaches faced similar conflicts, Imelda became interested in doing something about this problem. She was interested in proposing a program that the athletic and counseling departments of her school could develop to help women athletes with the value conflicts they were experiencing as a consequence of these pressures.

Imelda's goal was to encourage the coaches and counselors to help women athletes who were experiencing value conflicts in a traditional community to conceptualize these conflicts. In addition, Imelda proposed that coaches and counselors develop plans to intervene with parents and other members of the athletes' families to lessen value conflicts.

The therapist asked Imelda to identify someone in her social environment who might be interested in working on the problem with her. Imelda decided on one of the Hispanic women coaches whom she had gotten to know well during the match homework assignment. Imelda remembered the coach telling her that she had also faced opposition from parents and grandparents when she first showed interest in sports.

The therapist asked Imelda to consider what the majority of those coaches and counselors, who could play an important role in intervention with women athletes in conflict, wanted out of life. Imelda could speculate about her coaches' goals, but since she only knew two of the four counselors, she was limited in her knowledge about their life objectives. She said:

> I know most of the coaches want us to concentrate and keep our minds on the game. They always talk about how being distracted hurts our game plan. I know all of the assistant coaches would like to become head coach in a school; some of them would even like to be coaches in college some day. The two counselors I know are good fans of the women's teams; they always come to our games. I know one of them is working on her doctor's degree; the other one likes to read a lot about sports sociology and psychology and stuff like that because she helped me out with a term paper that I did on women in sports.

Imelda thought of ways to encourage the coaches and counselors to work together to develop a program of lectures and workshops addressing value conflicts often faced by women athletes in a traditional community and of intervention with the athletes and their families. She decided to approach the coach she had chosen as her ally to see if she would be willing to work on this with her.

Imelda would prepare a script that she would use in trying to enlist the support of her coach. The therapist and Imelda discussed the content of the script and the broad outline of the presentation to be made to the coaching staff and to the head counselor.

Because Imelda was working on developing her field independent learning and problem-solving and communication styles, Imelda and the therapist decided that she would prepare the script on her own and bring it to the next therapy session, so they could discuss and role-play it. After the role-playing exercise she would modify the script as necessary.

Details for the implementation of her homework assignment, empathy projection, and feeling awareness exercises as discussed in previous chapters were followed.

Once Imelda gained the support of her coach, they developed a plan for approaching the coaching staff. The head coach, in turn, approached the head of the counseling department for the final development and implementation of the intervention program.

Harold as Educator. A source of great frustration for Harold and his partners was that their branch plant in southern California was having employee turnover problems. This was one of the reasons why Harold had not felt confident that his company was on solid financial footing. After becoming familiar with the cultural styles component of the flex theory, Harold concluded that the on-site observations he had made, along with the reports from managers at the plant, could be explained in terms of cultural and cognitive styles conflicts between a predominantly Anglo supervisory staff and employees who were mainly Hispanic in origin.

Harold's goal was to help his partners conceptualize the turnover problem in this plant as a result of cultural and cognitive conflicts between the managers, the supervisory staff, and the employees.

Harold identified a friend from college who was a professor in the business school of an East Coast university. When Harold asked him for advice, his friend suggested a number of references in the management literature which addressed employee satisfaction problems relating to mismatch of supervisor and worker styles.

The therapist asked Harold to consider what his partners wanted out of life. Harold said, "Right now it's stabilizing things in the southern California plant. We can't move on to decide on new product development until things settle down there. They are all upset, because they don't understand what is happening over there."

Harold suggested developing a presentation for a directors' meeting where he could discuss the issues described in the references his professor friend had recommended. He would try to get his partners' backing in hiring a consultant who could assist them in resolving the problem.

Since Harold was learning how to use a field sensitive approach to learning and problem solving, the therapist and he worked on the script together. The script they developed used a field independent approach to communication and teaching to match the preferred cognitive style of Harold's partners. The script included identifying and defining the problem, and reviewing the literature Harold had read at his friend's suggestion. Further, the script called for Harold to distribute copies of some of the references he had read. Harold then presented a plan for training supervisors to be aware of cultural and cognitive preferred styles in those they supervise, and volunteered to direct the training efforts.

Assuming the role of educator includes the following techniques and procedures:

- identification of individual or institutional change goal
- identification of ally
- presentation of idea to ally
- changes in idea suggested by ally discussed with therapist
- empathy projection
- development of script
- role playing script with therapist
- enactment of script
- script is implemented and evaluated
- results of assessment are discussed with therapist.

Troy as Multicultural Peer Counselor. Several of Troy's African-American peers whom he had tutored talked about dropping out of school. Troy became even more conscious of the dropout problem among minority students after he watched a videotape on Hispanic drop-outs during one of his classes. In discussions with the therapist, Troy formulated a plan to develop a peer counseling program aimed at dropout prevention for African-American students at his school.

In the process of thinking about people who might be able to help him in implementing his plan, Troy decided that he would approach his cousin who was enrolled in a nearby university and who was active in the African-American studies program there.

Troy's empathy projection exercise was to figure out what his African-American friends who were experiencing trouble in school wanted out of life. Troy discussed this with his cousin, reviewed the videotape he had seen in class, and studied articles he found at the African-American studies library at the state university. Troy concluded that most of the reasons for dropping out of school had to do with alienation both from school personnel and from parents. The most consistent report by those at risk for leaving school early was, "No one cares whether I stay in school or not."

Troy resolved to invite his friends to go on a tour of the university sponsored by his cousin's African-American fraternity. His objective was to get the students interested in a university education and to form a mentor-type relationship between the fraternity members and the potential dropouts.

Troy worked on this project on his own in order to achieve increased development in the field independent learning and problem-solving style. He developed a script for approaching the leader of the disaffected students concerning his plan.

In the therapy session after Troy had drafted his script, he and the therapist discussed the script and role-played it. The therapist played the role of an untrusting African-American peer who felt patronized by Troy's intervention efforts. Some changes were made in the script and it was finalized. Using empathy projection and feeling awareness, Troy then decided on the details for the homework assignment.

Harold as Multicultural Peer Counselor. Harold's involvement in professional societies in several of the communities in the Bay Area of Northern California, led him to conclude that many of his colleagues were in crisis because they felt "burned out" and bored with their jobs.

These were professionals in their late 20s and early 30s who, despite the fact that they had achieved success in their professions, had become increasingly disillusioned with their work. Most were experiencing stress and confusion, and several of them were considering returning to college to pursue career interests they had abandoned earlier in their lives.

This struck a familiar chord in Harold, and he decided he wanted to do something about it. His preliminary conversations with some of these colleagues in crisis indicated that most of them did not want to go into psychotherapy or counseling, partly because of the stigma of seeking help and partly because they felt that this was something they should do on their own.

When Harold discussed his observations with the therapist, they arrived at the idea of having Harold look into the possibility of forming a support group for technical professionals suffering from burn-out. Specifically, the goal was to form such a group for professionals who were considering career changes because of burn-out and because of a perceived lack of meaning in their lives.

The therapist suggested that Harold contact a professor at one of the medical schools in the Bay Area who had developed a support group for burn-out among his colleagues. After talking to the professor, Harold refined his ideas and enlisted the support of two of his closest friends in one of the professional organizations in which he was a member. Together they approached the governing board of the organization for sponsorship and financial support for their idea.

The next step was for Harold to develop a script for presenting the support group idea to the officers of the organization. Since Harold was developing a field sensitive learning and problem-solving style, the therapist encouraged him to develop the script in cooperation with his friends in the organization.

Through discussions with his collaborators, Harold learned that the preferred styles of the officers of the organization were modern with respect to culture, but mixed with respect to cognitive styles. Harold and the therapist thus decided to modify the script to reflect this knowledge. The therapist alternated between playing an officer who was field independent and one who was field sensitive in order to allow Harold to prepare answers to questions emanating from either perspective.

Harold's homework assignment was completed in cooperation with his two friends. A final step was to implement and evaluate the script.

Encouraging the client to assume the role of multicultural peer counselor includes the following techniques and procedures:

- identification of individual change goal;
- development of preliminary plan with therapist;
- identification of resource people or institutions;
- identification of ally(ies), discussion of plan with ally(ies) and making changes suggested by ally(ies);
- developing a script for presentation of plan to "power holders";
- role playing script with therapist;
- making plans for enacting the script;
- enacting the script and assessing its effectiveness; and
- discussing results of assessment with therapist.

Wanda as a Multicultural Ambassador. Wanda had noted that many of the mid-level supervisors in her unit were experiencing problems of low productivity in their departments because of low morale resulting from ethnic or racial conflicts among their workers. She observed in visits to their departments that there was little or no cross-ethnic or racial socializing during lunch hours or coffee breaks; she observed the workers congregating in homogenous ethnic and racial groups.

Discussions with some of the supervisors led Wanda to discover that there had been confrontations among the workers because of ethnic slurs and other insults. She decided to work with her supervisors to develop a program for multicultural understanding and cooperation.

Wanda's goal was to work with mid-level supervisors and union representatives to develop multicultural awareness programs which could become part of the company's training program. A portion of time allocated for training was to be devoted to speakers and films which addressed negative stereotypes and to workshops concentrating on multicultural cooperation and understanding. The therapist directed Wanda through the same steps that Harold had followed in his peer counseling project.

Troy as Multicultural Ambassador. After having heard what his African-American peers had to say during their heart-to-heart talks with the members of his cousin's fraternity, Troy concluded that one of their major complaints was that they did not feel a part of the day-to-day life at school. They did not find validation of their interests and their cultures in the school curriculum and activities. Thus, he came on the idea that what was needed at his school was a multicultural awareness week.

Troy's goal was to involve students of the different ethnic groups at his school in making a proposal to the administration that they institute a cultural awareness week during which there would be activities and programs oriented towards better understanding and cooperation between members of different ethnic and racial groups. Another goal of the program would be to highlight the contributions of members of minority groups to American society, and to include this information as a permanent addition to the history and science curriculum at the school. The therapist led Troy through the same steps he had used with Harold and Wanda.

In summary, assuming the role of multicultural ambassador includes the following techniques and procedures:

- identification of institutional problem;
- development of plan with therapist;
- implementation of plan; and
- assessment of plan and discussion of results with therapist.

An Overview

The Multicultural Model of Psychotherapy differs from traditional models of personality change because one of its principle goals is client empowerment. The objectives of client activism and empowerment address a major concern which "the different" have had about traditional models of psychotherapy—that those models tend to encourage conformity and assimilation to the values and life styles of the "power structure." The activist-change agent phase of multicultural therapy transforms the client from a passive, alienated victim into an active participant helping to mold a society in which there is respect for, and sensitivity towards, cultural and individual differences.

SUMMARY

The final phase of multicultural therapy completes the task of client empowerment begun in the initial phase of counseling. This phase of therapy gives the client a role in changing institutions, in helping others, and in educating them in the concepts of personality flex and in the strategies of multicultural psychotherapy. Most important, it introduces them to the role of ambassador for a multicultural society of peace and cooperation.

Chapter 11

Couples Counseling

When the Multicultural Model of Psychotherapy is used in couples counseling, the focus of therapy is on individual differences in cultural and cognitive styles—the root source of many conflicts and misunderstandings occurring between partners. Therapy is directed at helping the clients to understand mismatch in communication, interpersonal relationship, motivation, learning and problem-solving, and teaching-parenting-supervisory and counseling styles. The partners then learn to match each other's preferred styles and to help one another to develop the flexibility in values and cognitive styles that can improve their level of satisfaction with the relationship.

The multicultural model is also sensitive to the fact that environmental forces and demands play a major role in the degree of satisfaction experienced by the partners in a relationship. Demands by jobs or careers, people, and institutions can produce strains in a relationship that are often manifested as rigidity in cultural and cognitive styles and/or as the triggering of developmental trends in cognitive and cultural styles which can lead to mismatch between partners who were previously well matched.

The cultural component of the multicultural model focuses on values match and mismatch. As such, it is useful for working with ethnically or racially mixed couples, or with partners who may be of the same culture and race but whose backgrounds are different in terms of socioeconomic, religious, regional, or family variables.

Specifically there are four major goals:

1. To make partners aware of match and mismatch areas or domains in their relationship;
2. To teach partners how to use the flex theory of personality and the Multicultural Model of Psychotherapy and Counseling to analyze conflicts associated with mismatch;

3. To teach both partners to match each other's preferred styles and to develop the flexibility which they will need to negotiate effectively with each other; and
4. To teach the partners to change environmental demands that are affecting the relationship and causing disharmony.

CASE HISTORY

This chapter describes how the Multicultural Model of personality change was used in conducting couples counseling with a couple whose members were from different ethnic groups. Wanda, whose case is one of the four highlighted in previous chapters, participated in counseling with her husband, Javier. Couples counseling was done during the same period of time Wanda was undergoing individual therapy.

Wanda and Javier: A History of the Relationship

As was discussed in chapter 4, Wanda and Javier had been married for eight years. They met after graduation from college when they were working for the same state agency. Although Wanda had grown up in a more modernistic sociocultural environment, she was attracted to the emotional closeness in Javier's extended family and by Javier's strong familial orientation.

For Javier, who had grown up in an urban-traditional Hispanic cultural environment, Wanda represented independence and assertiveness with a strong familial orientation, characteristics which he had always wanted in a partner.

The couple remembered that the initial years of their marriage were characterized by harmony and happiness: Wanda had left her full-time job and assumed the role of the traditional mother, taking primary responsibility for the home and the couples' two children (born in the third and fourth years of the marriage). In those early years of their marriage, Wanda had accepted small consulting contracts, working from an office at home.

Things changed drastically for the family in the sixth year of marriage when Wanda began working full-time as a mid-level manager in a large company. The couple's conflicts centered on the fact that Wanda did not feel supported in her career goals by Javier. Both Javier and the children felt that Wanda was devoting too much time to her work.

In the process of doing the initial individual session with Wanda, it became obvious to the therapist and to Wanda that the problems in her marriage and family were critical to her psychological adjustment. When

Wanda and the therapist began to identify her therapy goals during the second session of individual counseling, they decided that she would approach Javier about the possibility of his participating in couples counseling with her. What follows is a description of the process followed in couples counseling sessions with Javier and Wanda.

Session 1: The therapist greeted Javier and Wanda in the waiting room. Wanda introduced her husband to the therapist. Javier addressed the therapist by his title and surname and the therapist responded by addressing Javier formally, using his surname.

After Javier and Wanda were seated, the therapist explained that during Wanda's individual therapy it became clear that couples counseling might be appropriate. The therapist asked Javier for his feelings or thoughts on the idea.

Javier responded, "I thought it was a good idea myself because I've felt for a long time that our relationship has been getting worse. I didn't know what to do about it."

Therapist (to Javier):   Do you have any concerns about the fact that Wanda will be in individual therapy with me while your couples counseling is in progress?

Javier (to therapist):   No, not as long as our marriage problems are discussed in our sessions so that I can take part in them.

Wanda (to therapist and Javier):   I think that's the major reason why we are doing the couples counseling—to discuss our problems together and to work them out.

Therapist (to Javier):   I would like you to know that if at any time you feel that you would like to be in individual counseling I would be very happy to discuss this with you.

Javier (to therapist):   I'm fine with that.

The brief introduction and explanation was followed by the administration of the Dyadic Adjustment Inventory. This scale was developed by Spanier (1976), and assesses the quality of marital and other dyads by asking both members to rate their degree of agreement and disagreement in several areas such as handling family finances, household tasks, and demonstrations of affection. It also asks for ratings of frequency of those times the couple have stimulating exchanges of ideas and laugh together, as well as asking them to rate the degree of happiness of their relationship, from perfect to extremely unhappy.

The therapist attempted to establish an atmosphere of acceptance in which the clients could feel free to report the problems they perceived in their relationship. As soon as Wanda and Javier completed the questionnaires, the therapist proceeded to develop an atmosphere of nonjudgmental acceptance, and of rapport with them. He gave each of them the opportunity to talk about problems in their marriage from their individual perspectives. He also laid some ground rules, making it clear that he would not permit interruptions or arguments during the course of each person's presentation.

The next step of the first session was a short discussion of the partners' perspectives on the relationship, and of the feedback on the results of the Dyadic Adjustment Inventory based on preliminary observations made by comparing the ratings made by each of the partners.

While the discussion between the partners was in progress, the therapist observed, made notes, and rated the behaviors which each member used in interacting with the other. The therapist kept the Preferred Cultural and Cognitive Styles Observation Checklists in front of him. He remained cognizant of the fact that in disordered relationships involving mismatch, the individual partners tend to adopt a false self in their interactions with each other.

Thus, in the first two sessions the partners were likely to use their false selves as they interacted with each other. However, as the clients respond to the nonjudgmental, "safe" atmosphere of multicultural couples counseling, it was expected that they would gradually adopt their preferred cultural and cognitive styles when they related to each other.

Following the discussion on the individual perceptions of problems in the relationship, the therapist asked the clients to complete two additional paper and pencil instruments; the BOLS—(Javier only, Wanda had already completed this instrument)—and the Family Attitudes Scale (see appendix L) to assess their preferred cultural and cognitive styles. While they completed these, the therapist did a more thorough comparison of responses given by the partners on the Dyadic Adjustment Scale, noting both areas of agreement and of disagreement in their relationship.

After the clients completed their questionnaires, the therapist introduced them to the principal concepts of the flex theory of personality and of the Multicultural Model of Psychotherapy. In making the presentation, he used the same approach employed with individual clients discussed in chapter 9.

The therapist used some of the results of his preliminary observations and those from the Dyadic Adjustment Scale to personalize some of the concepts for Javier, whose preferred cognitive style in the learning and problem-solving domain based on initial observations of his interactions with Wanda and the therapist, appeared to be field sensitive. The therapist also discussed some of the background research on the concepts to best match Wanda's more field independent style in the learning and problem-solving domain.

For example, to match Javier, the therapist said, "What the two of you have described with respect to the different ways in which you relate to your children indicates that you have different values with respect to parenting. You, Mr. M., tend to be more traditional, wanting your children to respect you and to see you as an authority figure. On the other hand, Wanda is more modernistic, allowing the children to make their own decisions and to learn from experience rather than from direct teaching."

The therapist concluded the session by telling the clients that he would give them feedback on the findings of the behavioral ratings he had made, and on the findings of the instruments they had taken during the second session.

He asked each of them to think of one domain in the relationship in which they would like their partner to match them during the week. Wanda indicated that she would play a game of Trivial Pursuit® with Javier and the children after dinner on two nights during the coming week. Javier agreed to allow Wanda one hour after coming home from work each evening to unwind and to shift from her work mode to her family mode.

The therapist asked both partners to keep individual records of the dates, times, and situations in which they experienced match and mismatch. Each was given several copies of a record form on which to describe the matches and mismatches they experienced. They were asked to complete these without consulting each other, in order to see if there would be differences in terms of individual perception of the experiences (a sample record form appears in appendix M).

In summary, the first session included the following techniques and procedures:

1. Initial match and introduction to the goals of couples counseling;
2. Administration of the Dyadic Adjustment Scale;
3. Establishment of an atmosphere of acceptance in which the clients could feel free to report the problems they perceive in their relationship, and in which they would feel free to express their preferred cultural and cognitive styles;
4. Short discussion of each partner's perspectives on the relationship, and of preliminary findings of the Dyadic Adjustment Scale, and observation of cognitive and cultural styles used in interacting with the partner and therapist;
5. Administration of the BOLS and Family Attitudes Scales;
6. Introduction of the flex theory of personality and of the Multicultural Model of Psychotherapy; and
7. Closure of the session and assignment of homework for the coming week.

Session 2: During the second session, the therapist continued to develop an atmosphere in which each partner could feel free to express concerns about the relationship as well as one in which each could assume the cultural and cognitive styles most reflective of their unique selves.

The therapist asked each of the clients to give him the forms on which they had recorded the experiences of match and mismatch for the week. He read these aloud, asking the clients to comment or to supply details. Examination of the match and mismatch experiences each had perceived as being most important included an explanation using the concepts of the flex theory of personality and of the Multicultural Model of Psychotherapy.

In those situations in which conflict had occurred, the therapist pointed out how attempts at match by either or both partners might have prevented conflict. For example, both Javier and Wanda agreed that the major mismatch experience of the week had occurred when they disagreed about whether or not one of the children should be allowed to visit a neighborhood friend before completing his homework. Wanda's preferred modern cultural orientation, and her preferred field independent orientation in parenting style was reflected in her position that children should be allowed to develop their own sense of responsibility.

Javier's traditional and field sensitive orientations, however, stressed the need to be firm and directive with the children. They had argued over their different orientations, with Wanda accusing Javier of being too controlling and Javier accusing her of not caring enough about the children. Application of concepts from the flex theory and the Multicultural Model led to negotiation between Wanda and Javier and to a better understanding of how conflict could have been avoided.

Each member of the couple reported on how well matched they had felt with respect to the match assignments for the week. The therapist helped the clients to understand how cultural and cognitive match had contributed to harmony in their interactions.

The therapist reported on the findings obtained with the different instruments he had given to the clients during the earlier session. He also shared the findings of his observations regarding preferred cultural and cognitive styles as follows:

> The ratings you made on the Dyadic Adjustment Scale indicate that you have good agreement on many domains of your relationship: religion, family finances, friends, philosophy of life, decision making, and household tasks. There are a number of areas in which you seem to have disagreement: demonstration of affection, ways of dealing with parents and in-laws, amount of time spent together, and career decisions.
>
> On the Bicognitive Orientation to Life Scale, Wanda scored as a preferred field independent with partial development of the field sensitive style in

interpersonal relationships and communication style domains. Javier's scores indicated a strong preference for field sensitivity in all domains, although he did show some development of field independence in the learning and problem-solving styles domain.

With respect to preferred cultural styles, you are well matched on religion and time orientation, but mismatched on definition of gender roles. Javier tends to be more traditional in this area, whereas Wanda tends to be more modernistic. The same is true for child-rearing orientation.

After a short discussion relating to the assessment findings, the therapist asked the clients to focus on the identification of goals to be achieved through couples counseling. Wanda and Javier agreed on three goals:

1. Understanding how value and cognitive style differences are related to the areas of greatest disagreement between them;
2. Attempting to achieve a better cognitive styles match in learning and problem-solving and in parenting styles; and
3. Attempting to match cultural styles in gender roles and in child rearing orientations.

The therapist focused on parenting styles and on values related to parenting. He concentrated on the major mismatch conflict situations reported by the clients in the initial stages of the session as he role-played with each of the clients, showing them how match and negotiation could have been accomplished. He followed these five steps:

1. Values conflict analysis for understanding cultural styles mismatch. First the therapist interpreted the differences in values reflected by the incident previously mentioned: "Wanda values independence; she feels that children should make their own decisions and be responsible for the consequences of those decisions. Javier, on the other hand, values discipline and feels that parents should be models for their children."

2. Arriving at values negotiation. The therapist led a discussion of these differences in values, asking the clients to attempt to negotiate. They both agreed that the other's values had some merit, concluding that their children needed to be independent and that they needed to learn that their decisions had consequences. They also agreed that discipline and guidance were important as a stage preceding the development of independence. Wanda and Javier decided that conflict between them could have been avoided had they been able to respect each others values, deciding for example that their family rule is that the children can either complete their homework before dinner and then watch an hour of television after dinner, or play for an hour before dinner and then do their homework during the time they would have watched television.

3. Cognitive styles conflict analysis for understanding mismatch. The therapist asked the clients to focus on cognitive styles in communication,

showing them how they could have matched each other more closely in this domain to avoid conflict.

4. Cognitive styles negotiation. As an example, the therapist pointed out that Javier could have been more to-the-point in his explanation to Wanda as to why he objected to her decision to allow the children to play before they completed their homework. Wanda, by the same token, could have been more expressive in her explanation for making the decision she had made.

5. Empathy projection. Finally the therapist asked the clients to practice empathy projection (see chapter 9) so that they could experience what it was like to be in their partner's shoes.

Under the direction of the therapist, the couple discussed another major mismatch situation which had occurred during the week. They used the same procedure as that used with the discussion of the first incidence of mismatch.

Taking into consideration the areas of cultural and cognitive styles in which the clients need to effect a better match, the therapist led the clients in an examination of their social environments (see chapter 10) for the purpose of identifying diversity challenges in which they could engage for the coming week.

Javier recalled that one of their son's Little League coaches seemed to be modernistic and field independent in his orientation as he worked with the children. Javier decided to make time to watch him while he worked with the members of the team during practice.

Wanda, remembered that one of Javier's older sisters was traditional and field sensitive in her child-rearing, and she decided to visit with her and observe her closely while she interacted with her children.

During the coming week, Wanda agreed to use a field sensitive style while communicating with Javier. Javier agreed to try to use a field independent style. The therapist suggested that they should both read Aaron Beck's *Love Is Never Enough* for ideas on communication match.

Session 2, in summary, included the following techniques and procedures:

- continued development of an atmosphere permitting expression of the true self;
- clients' reports of match and mismatch experiences for the past week;
- clients' reports of the degree of success with match assignments for the week;
- feedback from the therapist on the results of assessment;
- an analysis of cultural and cognitive match, and role playing to achieve match goals;
- homework match assignments for the coming week.

Session 3: The therapist began the third session by asking the clients to report on the degree of success they had achieved in their match assignments for the previous week. This was followed by reports on each partner's perception of the most significant mismatch incident of the week.

The therapist noted that both Wanda and Javier followed the steps for analysis and match which he had introduced during the previous session. He congratulated them on their efforts. The therapist also observed that both clients were interacting in a way that showed growth in cultural and cognitive match.

The major techniques introduced in Session 3 were script writing and role-playing for both match and negotiation. The match script was developed with the therapist selecting one of the areas of conflict identified by each of the clients in their discussions—Javier's belief that since Wanda had returned to work outside the home she had become cold and distant, and Wanda's belief that Javier had become too emotionally demanding and was not supportive of her career goals.

The therapist presented a scenario and asked each member of the couple to predict how the other would react in the following hypothetical situation: After Wanda has had her hour to unwind, Javier approaches her to tell her he would like to discuss a conflict he has experienced with one of his coworkers.

The therapist gave both Wanda and Javier a pad and asked them to predict what the other would say and do in this situation. When each had completed the task, the therapist asked them to take turns in reading their predictions out loud.

Javier: I wouldn't get much emotional support from Wanda. Instead of focusing on my hurt feelings, she would be objective and want me to give a lot of detail about what happened. Then she would interpret the incident as a misunderstanding between my colleague and me.

Wanda: Javier would get very emotional and would wind up confusing me with his description of the incident. Whenever he is angry or upset, he is not clear in what he communicates. He has a hard time getting to the point. Basically, I wouldn't know what he expected from me, and we would end up arguing.

Therapist: From a traditional cultural styles perspective, the one major thing which Javier seems to want is for Wanda to focus on his feelings. At least for the moment, he wants her to ignore the details of the incident.

From a cognitive styles point of view, the communication, human relations, and problem-solving style domains seem to be involved: When he is upset, Javier becomes field sensitive in his communication style and this mismatches your (looking at Wanda) preferred field independent style.

From the perspective of human relations style, Javier would like you to focus on his nonverbal communications and from the learning and problem-solving styles perspective, Javier would like for you to show sympathy and caring, and to let him know that you support him, that you want to help him to find a solution. This is a field sensitive approach. A field independent approach would be to analyze the situation in order to help him to understand why the conflict occurred.

The therapist then role-plays the script (taking the role of the opposite partner) with each client. When the role-playing is in progress, the partner whose role the therapist has taken observes and rates the behavior with the Preferred Cognitive and Cultural Styles Observation Checklists.

The next step involved discussing the observations made by the client, making changes, and repeating the role-playing with the changes incorporated. Both clients role-play the final script while the therapist observes and rates.

Following this exercise, the therapist reintroduces the same incident and asks the clients to write a negotiation script on their note pads—a script in which each of them was partially but not completely matched in their preferred styles. Each partner reads the negotiation scripts out loud.

Wanda: Culturally, I would be more traditional in listening and observing Javier's expression of feeling. I should tell him right away that I support him and stand behind him. Once he has settled down, I can use my field independent problem-solving style to help him analyze what happened.

Javier: I need to calm down before telling my troubles to Wanda. I could develop a little exercise for myself based on what I've learned from writing scripts. I could write down what happened and organize what I want to say so that I can use a field independent communication style when I actually communicate with her. However, I would still make it clear that I need and want her support.

The therapist and clients discussed the negotiation scripts. The clients then role-played them while the therapist observed and rated them using the observation instruments. Discussion followed the role-playing and changes in the scripts and behaviors were made as necessary. The session ended with homework assignments of match and diversity challenges for the coming week.

In summary, Session 3 included the following techniques and procedures:

- clients' reports of match and mismatch experiences for the past week;
- introduction of script writing and role-playing activities for match and negotiation;
- writing a match script for one of the major conflicts and role-playing that script; and
- writing a negotiation script and role-playing it.

Sessions 4 and 5: During these sessions, the therapist and clients continued with the development and role-playing of match and negotiation scripts.

Session 6: This session focused on environmental demands and forces that cause strain on the relationship. The first step was to identify these demands. The therapist began the discussion by reminding the clients about the three areas which appeared to be most affected by environmental forces as indicated by their responses on the Dyadic Adjustment Scale: (a) friends; (b) aims, goals, and things believed to be important; and (c) relating to parents and in-laws.

The therapist led Wanda and Javier in a discussion directed at identifying the exact nature of the demands and forces causing conflict. In the area of work and career, both partners expressed dissatisfaction: Javier was unhappy when Wanda's unit managers called her at home to discuss problems in their unit, while Wanda resented Javier's supervisor's attempts to pressure him into playing golf on weekends.

Another environmental force identified as affecting the couple was exerted by their friends: Javier's friends wanted him to meet them after work on Fridays for happy hour. Wanda was angered by this as she felt that it cut into the time she and Javier could spend together. Javier did not like to socialize with Wanda's friends because at times they made ethnic or racial jokes, which made him uneasy.

Parents and in-laws were also identified as a source of pressures for Wanda and Javier: Javier's parents pressured them to teach their children Spanish, and Wanda felt that they were too demanding on this subject. Wanda's parents accused Javier of encouraging the children to be too dependent on him.

Their children's demands also affected the couple's relationship. They complained to Javier that Wanda wasn't spending enough time with them anymore while they complained to Wanda that Javier was too strict with them.

After identifying these environmental forces, the therapist asked the couple to negotiate on their solutions. They agreed on compromises for a number of the problems. The negotiations included Wanda's asking her coworkers not to call her on weekends or after 9:00 p.m. on weekdays, and Javier agreed to tell his supervisor that he needed to spend more time with his family, and that he would only be available for golf every other weekend. Wanda agreed to confront her friends about their racial jokes, while Javier agreed to limit his Friday happy hour with his friends to every other weekend.

The next step in the sixth session of couples counseling involved an analysis of cultural and cognitive styles mismatch related to environmental pressures and demands. The therapist asked each partner to use their note pads to answer several questions: (a) In your opinion how are the demands and pressures of work and career changing the cultural styles of your partner. (b) How are these pressures changing his or her cognitive styles? and (c) How are you reacting to these changes? Upon completion, each partner read the answers aloud and discussed them.

Wanda: Ever since Javier took the job with the Hispanic firm he works for now, I feel that he has become more traditional in his values and more rigid in his definition of gender roles. He has also become more field sensitive in his cognitive style in the parenting area. He wants the children to do things exactly the way he wants; he has become more autocratic in his manner as a father and as a husband.

Javier: Since Wanda took her job as manager, I feel that she has lost interest in us as a family. She has become more self-centered. Her cognitive style has become very field independent—she lets the children make too many decisions on their own; they are too young and not ready for that.

Hearing the opinions of the partner regarding the changes resulting from their jobs and careers was enlightening for both Javier and Wanda. The discussion facilitated negotiation. They agreed that they would each make an attempt to be more flexible culturally and cognitively. They agreed that their relationship was more important than their careers, and they decided to be more conscious of how job and career demands were causing mismatch.

The sixth session ended after match and diversity challenge assignments were made for the coming week.

Session 6, in summary, included the following:

- identification of environmental demands and forces;
- discussion to discover the exact nature and impact of environmental forces and demands on the relationship;
- negotiation, discussion, and decisions;
- identification of specific cultural and cognitive developmental trends triggered by environmental forces and demands; and
- negotiation decisions.

Sessions 7, 8, and 9: During these three sessions the couple continued to practice techniques and procedures introduced in earlier sessions: analysis of mismatch experiences of the previous week, development of match and negotiation scripts, role-playing the scripts, development of strategies for controlling environmental pressures, and negotiating to keep those pressures and demands from leading to extreme cultural and cognitive styles mismatch. During Session 9, the Dyadic Adjustment Scale was re-administered, and the therapist completed observational ratings throughout the course of the session.

Session 10: During the tenth session, the therapist gave the couple feedback on the findings obtained from the re-administered Dyadic Adjustment Scale, comparing these to the findings from the first administration of the scale.

He reported the following to Wanda and Javier:

> I am happy to report that your recent ratings on the Dyadic Adjustment Scale show that there has been a substantial reduction in areas of disagreement in your relationship. Most impressive is the fact that you now show good agreement in the following areas: demonstration of affection, philosophy of life, major decision making, and career decisions. The ratings indicate that you are now communicating more effectively.
>
> There are certain areas of disagreement which remain, for example, the amount of time you spend together. You still need to identify more things you can do together and you need to make more time to be together. You both reported that you occasionally disagree about this. The ratings I made of your behaviors in the last session indicate that you are matching each other better on cultural styles: you are both flexing well in terms of traditional and modern values. Javier, however, is still showing a preference for traditional values, while Wanda seems to have a preference for modern values. Nevertheless, you are now much more sensitive to these differences, and I noticed several attempts to negotiate.
>
> I've also noticed that you are also negotiating well on cognitive styles, even though Javier is still preferred field sensitive, and Wanda is still preferred field independent. You have learned to match each other and to negotiate bicognitive orientations in the teaching and parenting, and learning and problem-solving domains.

A long discussion followed, but no major unresolved problems emerged. The therapist proceeded to terminate counseling, but made an appointment for one month hence for a follow-up session. He made it clear that he would be available for an earlier appointment should they feel it necessary.

Session 10, in summary, included the following:

- feedback on re-administered instruments
- termination, and agreeing on follow-up sessions.

Session 11: During the first follow-up session, Wanda and Javier completed the Dyadic Adjustment Scale again. The therapist compared their ratings, noting that there were now no areas of major disagreement in their reports.

The therapist asked each of them for their perceptions of the progress being made in their relationship. While they did report some major mismatch situations during the month since their last session, they agreed that they had been successful in negotiating them. The therapist scheduled another follow-up session six months hence and terminated the session.

Session 12: The second follow-up followed the same procedures used in session 11. As no problems surfaced, the therapist indicated that he saw no need for continued sessions. Wanda and Javier concurred. The therapist assured them that he was available should they need additional counseling.

SUMMARY

When the Multicultural Model is applied in couples counseling, the primary focus in on mismatch in values and in cognitive styles—the root source of many conflicts in relationships. In addition to teaching techniques and procedures which lead to match and negotiation, the therapist also helps the clients to identify external, or environmental, forces and demands. Environmental demands can cause dissatisfaction in the relationship and trigger the development of trends in values and cognitive styles which are also related to mismatch. The partners learn to control and negotiate with respect to the disrupting forces.

Chapter 12

Conclusions

Everyone has the potential to develop a multicultural orientation to life. However, as seen from examining the lives of Imelda, Harold, Troy, and Wanda, the sociocultural environment can impose barriers that make it difficult if not impossible to achieve cognitive and cultural flexibility.

What are the barriers to multicultural development? There are three major categories: pressures to conform, prejudice, and oppression. In general, these three types of barriers are conceptualized under what can be referred to as the politics of diversity. Politics of diversity are reflected in the dynamics of families, of institutions, and of societies. They reflect the messages, whether direct or indirect, passed on to individuals about the desirability of diversity versus ethnocentrism. Through these, the individual learns to view diversity as either positive or negative.

Different individuals are subjected to different barriers to multicultural development and to varying degrees of permeability of these barriers. The cases of Imelda and Harold best exemplify pressures to conform as barriers to multicultural development. Both were subjected to strong pressures to adopt cultural and cognitive styles which were different from those they preferred. They were encouraged by parents or parental figures to reject their unique selves and to conform to an imposed ideal.

Most individuals have experienced pressures to conform because of the prevalence of certain mythical ideals imposed by all societies, institutions, and families on their members (Brink, 1984). While these ideals vary from society to society, the following are examples of mainstream American mythical ideals:

- blonde, blue-eyed, white-skinned people are smarter than those who have darker complexions;
- men are better at business, science, and math than are women;

- engineers, physicians and lawyers are smarter than those who work in the social sciences or the arts; and
- it is better to be tall and thin than to be short and stocky.

Almost everyone has had these mythical ideals imposed on them to a certain degree. The result has been feelings of inferiority, because it is almost impossible to fit these ideals perfectly. Beyond limiting the individual, these mythical ideals prevent members of society from recognizing the value of the diversity around them, and from benefitting from it.

Prejudice was the most important barrier in the experiences of Wanda and Troy. Because Wanda was a woman and because Troy was African-American, they were made to feel unwanted and were given the message that they did not belong.

Through prejudicial practices, those who hold the power in institutions deny equality of status to people who are different from them. The message is: "You can only achieve the 'goodies' of society if you are like us. You can't be like us if your phenotype, your gender, your values, or your sexual preferences are not like ours."

Prejudice is destructive to the development of a positive politics of diversity (Castaneda, 1984), because it keeps members of different groups separated from each other, and because it promotes the idea that certain groups and cultures are superior to others.

Oppression is more destructive than the other two barriers. Not only are people pressured to be what they are not and kept from fully participating in society, but they are also exploited for being who they are as individuals (Ramirez, 1972).

In Harold's case the barrier was his father's refusal to accept his interest in the arts and his preferred personality style. His father's attempt to force him to be like his dead brother was oppressive to Harold.

For Imelda the barrier was her peers at school who would cheer her exploits on the basketball court but who would refuse to include her in their circle of friends because they felt she was not feminine enough.

A society which hopes to understand, to nurture, and to value its diversity has to be able to identify and eliminate the barriers preventing multicultural development in its institutions and in its members.

How can social scientists and educators encourage the development of positive politics of diversity in families, institutions, and societies? Three approaches may move toward that direction.

First would be the development of social science paradigms and research and intervention techniques which are truly based on individual and cultural differences. For example, Ramirez (1983) proposed a theory, along with a set of research strategies and intervention approaches, which is based on the principles of multiculturalism.

In addition, the rise of a positive politics of diversity is reflected in the development of community psychology intervention programs in third world countries. These programs focus on the empowerment of heretofore disenfranchised peoples. In the last few years, the writings as well as the research and development work of psychologists in Latin America and the Carribean have shown a trend towards empowerment programs.

For example, Almeida (1984) and his colleagues, an interdisciplinary team of social scientists, are working in three rural communities in the state of Puebla in Mexico. The team's objective is to provide assistance in community development without producing radical changes in the native cultures of the region. Part of the program involves the development of a marketing program whereby local artisans and farmers can sell their products without losing profits to middlemen.

Other members of the team are working with school personnel to upgrade curriculum and instruction techniques. The programs are actively encouraging parental participation in the education of their children.

The Uruguayan psychologist Jose Varela (1975) has applied a community psychology perspective to intervention into the social challenges in his country; he refers to it as "social technology." The Venezuelan psychologist Jose Miguel Salazar (1981) has been advocating the development of a social psychology reflecting the historical and political realities of the cultures of Latin America.

Another Venezuelan psychologist, Moritza Montero (1979), has called for the development of a community psychology which has as its primary goal assisting people in the development of their communities. An overview of social psychology in Latin American by Marin (1975) indicated that recent developments there represent a good amalgamation of scientific objectivity with a definite commitment to the solution of social problems. He concluded that applied social psychology is the most important area of concentration in Latin American psychology.

The third approach is the development of multicultural educational programs. These programs address the goal of teaching children and adolescents to recognize, to respect, and to learn from individual and cultural differences in order to prevent the development of negative stereotypes, and vulnerability to coercion by the mythical ideals of society.

Ramirez and Castaneda (1974) and Cox, Macaulay and Ramirez (1982) described a cognitive flex-multicultural program evolved from the perspective of Hispanic-Americans. Hale-Benson (1986) described a multicultural educational program specifically relevant to African-Americans.

The challenge for social scientists and educators in encouraging the evolution of a positive politics of diversity is indeed great. It will be difficult to eradicate notions of superiority and inferiority in the perceptions of individuals, groups, cultures, and nations. Equally challenging is overcoming negative stereotypes and suspicions different peoples hold regarding others. However, the rewards of a positive politics of diversity are high. It is multicultural orientations to life that can lead to maximum development of the personality, and to peace and cooperation in the world.

For the four people whose lives we have followed in this book, a multicultural perspective and a flexible orientation towards life were the keys to self-acceptance, to greater awareness of how the environment was affecting their lives and to the further development of their potential. A multicultural orientation to life gave Imelda, Harold, Troy, and Wanda the empowerment they needed to gain increased control over their own destinies. It also furnished the tools they needed to help the people and societal institutions in their environments to achieve greater multicultural awareness.

Furthermore, multicultural counseling and therapy opened up different possibilities for growth and development in their lives and provided them with the coping techniques they needed to accept their uniqueness and to learn from, and to relate more effectively to, the diversity around them.

Imelda became more assertive and outgoing. This resulted in the development of a circle of friends and mentors who were available as a support system to her, and who were also good models and sources of increased knowledge as she strove to develop flexibility in her values and cognitive styles.

As she began to work closely with the student council in her school, her efforts in that organization gave students a greater voice in making changes in the curriculum and teaching approaches, as well as in counseling services offered to female athletes. Her relationships with her parents and grandparents improved as she learned to match their values and behaviors more effectively. They in turn became more supportive of her interests, and more responsive to her requests for treatment equal to that given to her half sister.

Harold's relationship with his family improved dramatically. He and his wife developed a satisfying and productive partnership in the art gallery they opened. The family's mutual interests in photography and travel brought them together as they had never been before. Harold came to recognize that he had been relating to his own children in much the same way as his father had related to him. In response, he became more supportive of their interests and activities while at the same time giving them the opportunity to develop their own unique styles.

Harold was also successful in convincing his business partners of the need to develop a new product line in graphic art software. This revitalized his interest in the firm. He felt more enthusiastic about playing the role of charismatic leader, and about developing a sense of community in the firm.

For the first time since he was a student in middle school, Harold began to play the piano. This renewed interest in music helped him to reestablish his close relationship with his mother. His efforts at initiating the support groups in Silicon Valley for technical professionals who were experiencing symptoms of "burn out" was also a source of great satisfaction for him.

Harold was happy to have been able to make peace with his father and to establish a meaningful friendship with him. His ability to match his father's style eventually led his father to empathize with him, and to apologize for trying to transform him into the image of his dead brother.

Troy came to feel more comfortable as an African-American adolescent in a conservative Ango-dominated school and community. He became an effective student leader and was respected by both his African-American and Anglo peers. He succeeded in encouraging the development of racially mixed peer groups both in the school and in the community.

His efforts to match his parents' styles resulted in improved relations with them. His mother became less demanding and more supportive of his creative writing and of his efforts at improving cultural sensitivity at school.

Troy continued to be interested in science fiction and wrote several short stories focusing on how acceptance of cultural and racial differences were the keys to peace and cooperation in initial encounters between peoples of different worlds. His preliminary efforts in drop-out prevention were supported by the counseling department of his school and by one of the African-American assistant coaches. A joint program involving tutoring by college students and organized visits to the university was developed in conjunction with the African-American student organization at the state university.

When the therapist last had contact with Troy, Troy was in the last half of his senior year at high school and was making plans to attend a private university on the West Coast to study journalism and political science. He was planning to take courses in African-American studies and to do volunteer work with minority children in schools with high drop-out rates.

Wanda's efforts to create a sense of community among her management colleagues had a major impact on the company she worked for, and earned her a promotion to vice-president of human resources. Her relationships with Javier and with her children improved. They began to do more things as a family. Javier and Wanda became leaders of a weekend retreat program for couples who were experiencing marital problems. Wanda became active in Adult Children of Alcoholics support groups. She also became a major advocate for primary prevention programs for addictive disorders in businesses and schools.

Imelda, Harold, Troy, and Wanda were able to develop the flexibility of personality and world view they needed to function effectively in a diverse society. They were also able to effect changes in their environments and to assist others who, like themselves, felt mismatched to situations and to people around them.

These four clients had a profound effect on the therapist: through them he learned that the definition of pluralism and culture that he was using when he first began his work in multicultural therapy was too limiting and static. He learned that the "differentness" experience is not limited to members of cultural, ethnic, and gender minority groups. Most importantly, he learned to look beyond the superficials, the external characteristics of differentness, and to look for the internal expressions and signs of uniqueness.

As a therapist, he learned to examine his value system and his preferred cognitive style and to understand how these affect the clients with whom he works. As a researcher, the therapist rediscovered the value of intensive study of the individual case. He came to understand that the life history is the royal road to the realization that peoples' experiences are valuable lessons for arriving at understandings about the meaning of life.

It reminded him of the words that his colleague and mentor Al Castaneda considered representative of the philosophy of life he had developed from the experience of growing up in the ethnically diverse Mission District of San Francisco in the 1930s and 40s—"You can learn something from everyone because every person has, through their life experiences, discovered some truths about the meaning of life." These words are an effective statement of the principal mission of multicultural counseling and psychotherapy.

Appendix A

Scoring Procedure for the Multicultural Experience Inventory

The Multicultural Experience Inventory (MEI) is comprised of two types of items. Type A items are scored so that a response of "All Hispanics" or "All Anglos" (alternatives one and five, respectively) receives one point; responses of either "Mostly Hispanics" or "Mostly Anglos" (alternatives two and four respectively) receive two points; responses of "Hispanics and Anglos about equal" (alternative three) receive three points. Hence, higher scores are indicative of a greater degree of multiculturalism. Items numbered 33 through 49 are Type A items.

There are two categories of Type A items: historical and contemporary. Items 35, 36, 37, 39, 42, 44, 46, and 47 are historical. Items 33, 34, 38, 40, 41, 43, 45, 48, and 49 are contemporary. In some research projects historical items may be just as important as contemporary ones, while in other projects contemporary items may carry more weight. Researchers will have to make their own decisions, basing their choices on the principal hypothesis(es) of their study.

Type B items are arranged in a Likert-type format with alternatives ranging from "Very often" (alternative one) to "Never" (alternative five). The eight Type B items are arranged into four pair combinations, each pair contrasting the individual's degree of participation in Anglo and Hispanic cultures in a given domain. A response of either "Very often" or "Often" on the two items comprising any pair combination receives three points. Paired responses including any combination of "Very often," and "Seldom" or "Occasionally" receive two points. All other pair combinations receive one point. The higher the score the greater the person's degree of multicultural orientation is judged to be. The following pairs are Type B items: 50 and 51, 52 and 54, 53 and 55, and 56 and 57.

A total multicultural score is obtained by summing the points awarded for Type A and Type B items. Since there are seventeen Type A items and four Type B pairs, sixty-three is the maximum possible value, indicating the highest level of multicultural orientation. Decisions as to what scores are considered to indicate high, medium, or low multiculturalism must be made relative to the region of the country in which the investigation is performed, and to the population being studied. Environments vary with respect to degree of opportunity for multicultural development.

MEI Part 1

1. Name _____

2. Address: _____   _____
   (number, street)   (city, state, zip code)

3. Phone Numbers: *day* _____   *evening:* _____

4. Gender (check one): ___ male   ___ female

5. Age: ___

6. Date of Birth: _____   _____   _____
                   month   day   year

7. Place of Birth: _____   _____   _____
                    city   state   country

8. Father's Place of Birth: _____   _____   _____
                             city   state   country

9. Mother's Place of Birth: _____   _____   _____
                             city   state   country

10. Please indicate the ethnic background of the following persons (check where applicable):

	Yourself	Father	Mother
Hispanic			
African–American			
Anglo/White			
Asian–American			
Native–American			
Other (specify)			

11. What school do you now attend? _____

12. What is your major? _____

13. What is your class standing? (check one): ___ freshman
    ___ sophomore   ___ junior   ___ senior   ___ graduate student

14. Even if you are not currently active, what is your religious background? (check one):
    ___ Catholic   ___ Protestant   ___ Jewish   ___ Other: _____
                                                                (please specify)

15. How many years have you lived in the United States? _____

16. Have you lived in a country other than the United States? (check one):
    ____ yes   ____ no

    16a. If yes, in what country: _____

    16b. For how many years? _____

17. Are you a resident of the state in which you now attend school? (check one):
    ____ yes   ____ no

    17a. If yes, how many years have you been a resident? _____

    17b. If no, of which state are you a resident? _____

18. Have you ever lived in a state other than the one in which you now attend school? (check one):
    ____ yes   ____ no

    18a. If yes, in which state(s)? _____

    18b. For how many years? _____

19. Where did you spend the first 15 years of your life? (list all places):

    _____

20. What is the city, town, or community that you consider home?

    _____

    20a. Approximately how many miles is this place from the Mexican border? (check one):
    ____ 0–100   ____ 101–200   ____ 201–300   ____ 301–400
    ____ 401–500   ____ 501–750   ____ 751–1000   ____ 1,001–2,000
    ____ more than 2,000 miles

    20b. How would you describe this community? (check one):
    ____ rural   ____ semi-rural   ____ semi-urban   ____ urban

21. What language(s) does your father speak? _____

22. What language(s) does your mother speak? _____

23. What language(s) do you speak? _____

24. How well do you speak Spanish? (check one):
    ____ very fluently   ____ somewhat fluently   ____ can communicate basic ideas

___ can speak only some basic words and phrases
___ can understand it but can't speak it   ___ no knowledge of Spanish

25. What language(s) do your parents speak at home? _____

26. What language(s) do you speak at home? _____

27. How many of the following do you have? younger brothers:___
younger sisters: ___ older brothers: ___ older sisters: ___

28. What is the highest level of education achieved by each of your parents? (check one in each column):

	Father	Mother
Less than high school		
Some high school		
High school graduate		
Some college		
College graduate		
Advanced degree (for example, Ph.D., M.D.)		

29. Parents' occupation: (If retired, deceased, or unemployed, indicate former occupation)

29a. Father's occupation: _____

29b. Mother's occupation: _____

30. What is your marital status? (check one): ___ never married
___ divorced   ___ married
___ separated   ___ widowed

30a. If you are (were) married, what is (was) the ethnic background of your spouse? (check one):
___ Hispanic   ___ African-American
___ Asian-American   ___ Native-American
___ Anglo/White   ___ Other: _____
(Specify)

31. Do you have relatives who live in another country(ies)? (check one):

   ____ yes   ____ no

   31a. If yes, in which country(ies)? _____

32. Do you have close friends who live in another country(ies)? (check one):

   ____ yes   ____ no

   32a. If yes, in which one(s)? _____

MEI Part 2 (Check appropriate choices)

Type A Items

33. The ethnic composition of the neighborhood in which I now live is:
   ____ 1. All Hispanic
   ____ 2. Mostly Hispanic
   ____ 3. Hispanic and Anglo, about equal
   ____ 4. Mostly Anglo
   ____ 5. All Anglo
   ____ 6. Other _____

34. At present, my close friends are:
   ____ 1. All Hispanics
   ____ 2. Mostly Hispanics
   ____ 3. Hispanics and Anglos, about equal
   ____ 4. Mostly Anglos
   ____ 5. All Anglos
   ____ 6. Other _____

35. In high school, my close friends were:
   ____ 1. All Hispanics
   ____ 2. Mostly Hispanics
   ____ 3. Hispanics and Anglos, about equal
   ____ 4. Mostly Anglos
   ____ 5. All Anglos
   ____ 6. Other _____

36. The ethnic background of the people I have dated is:
   ____ 1. All Hispanic
   ____ 2. Mostly Hispanic

____ 3. Hispanic and Anglo, about equal
____ 4. Mostly Anglo
____ 5. All Anglo
____ 6. Other _____

37. The people with whom I have established close and meaningful relationships have been:
    ____ 1. All Hispanics
    ____ 2. Mostly Hispanics
    ____ 3. Hispanics and Anglos, about equal
    ____ 4. Mostly Anglos
    ____ 5. All Anglos
    ____ 6. Other _____

38. When I am with my friends, I usually attend functions where the people are:
    ____ 1. All Hispanics
    ____ 2. Mostly Hispanics
    ____ 3. Hispanics and Anglos, about equal
    ____ 4. Mostly Anglos
    ____ 5. All Anglos
    ____ 6. Other _____

39. My childhood friends who visited in my home and related well to my parents were:
    ____ 1. All Hispanics
    ____ 2. Mostly Hispanics
    ____ 3. Hispanics and Anglos, about equal
    ____ 4. Mostly Anglos
    ____ 5. All Anglos
    ____ 6. Other _____

40. My close friends at work are:
    ____ 1. All Hispanics
    ____ 2. Mostly Hispanics
    ____ 3. Hispanics and Anglos, about equal
    ____ 4. Mostly Anglos
    ____ 5. All Anglos
    ____ 6. Other _____

41. I enjoy going to gatherings at which the people are:
    ____ 1. All Hispanics
    ____ 2. Mostly Hispanics
    ____ 3. Hispanics and Anglos, about equal
    ____ 4. Mostly Anglos

___ 5. All Anglos
___ 6. Other _____

42. The people who have most influenced me in my education have been:
   ___ 1. All Hispanics
   ___ 2. Mostly Hispanics
   ___ 3. Hispanics and Anglos, about equal
   ___ 4. Mostly Anglos
   ___ 5. All Anglos
   ___ 6. Other _____

43. When I study with others, I usually study with:
   ___ 1. All Hispanics
   ___ 2. Mostly Hispanics
   ___ 3. Hispanics and Anglos, about equal
   ___ 4. Mostly Anglos
   ___ 5. All Anglos
   ___ 6. Other _____

44. In the job(s) I have had, my close friends have been:
   ___ 1. All Hispanics
   ___ 2. Mostly Hispanics
   ___ 3. Hispanics and Anglos, about equal
   ___ 4. Mostly Anglos
   ___ 5. All Anglos
   ___ 6. Other _____

45. When I am involved in group discussions where I am expected to participate, I prefer a group made up of:
   ___ 1. All Hispanics
   ___ 2. Mostly Hispanics
   ___ 3. Hispanics and Anglos, about equal
   ___ 4. Mostly Anglos
   ___ 5. All Anglos
   ___ 6. Other _____

46. The ethnic affiliation of the priests, ministers, nuns, or other clergypersons who have influenced my life have been:
   ___ 1. All Hispanics
   ___ 2. Mostly Hispanics
   ___ 3. Hispanics and Anglos, about equal
   ___ 4. Mostly Anglos
   ___ 5. All Anglos
   ___ 6. Other _____

47. The teachers and counselors with whom I have had the closest relationships have been:
___ 1. All Hispanics
___ 2. Mostly Hispanics
___ 3. Hispanics and Anglos, about equal
___ 4. Mostly Anglos
___ 5. All Anglos
___ 6. Other _____

48. When I discuss personal problems or issues, I discuss them with:
___ 1. All Hispanics
___ 2. Mostly Hispanics
___ 3. Hispanics and Anglos, about equal
___ 4. Mostly Anglos
___ 5. All Anglos
___ 6. Other _____

49. When I write poetry or other personal material, I write in:
___ 1. Spanish only
___ 2. Mostly Spanish
___ 3. Spanish and English, about equal
___ 4. Mostly English
___ 5. English only

Type B Items

50. I attend functions which are predominantly Anglo in nature:
___ 1. Extensively
___ 2. Frequently
___ 3. Occasionally
___ 4. Seldom
___ 5. Never

51. I attend functions which are predominantly Hispanic in nature:
___ 1. Extensively
___ 2. Frequently
___ 3. Occasionally
___ 4. Seldom
___ 5. Never

52. I visit the home of Anglos (not relatives):
___ 1. Very often
___ 2. Often
___ 3. Occasionally
___ 4. Seldom
___ 5. Never

53. I invite Anglos to my home (not relatives):
    ___ 1. Very often
    ___ 2. Often
    ___ 3. Occasionally
    ___ 4. Seldom
    ___ 5. Never

54. I visit the homes of Hispanics (not relatives):
    ___ 1. Very often
    ___ 2. Often
    ___ 3. Occasionally
    ___ 4. Seldom
    ___ 5. Never

55. I invite Hispanics to my home (not relatives):
    ___ 1. Very often
    ___ 2. Often
    ___ 3. Occasionally
    ___ 4. Seldom
    ___ 5. Never

56. I visit relatives and/or close friends in Mexico or other countries in
    Latin America:
    ___ 1. Very often (about once a month)
    ___ 2. Often (several times a year)
    ___ 3. Occasionally (once or twice a year)
    ___ 4. Seldom (less than once a year)
    ___ 5. Never

57. Relatives and/or close friends from Mexico or other countries of
    Latin America visit me:
    ___ 1. Very often (about once a month)
    ___ 2. Often (several times a year)
    ___ 3. Occasionally (once or twice a year)
    ___ 4. Seldom (less than once a year)
    ___ 5. Never

Appendix B

Instructions for Scoring the Traditionalism Modernism Inventory

The T items are the following: 3, 4, 5, 8, 9, 11, 12, 13, 19, 20, 21, 22, 23, 28, 30, 31, 34, 36, 37, and 39. All the rest are M items. Add the scores for T items and the scores for M items. Then, substract M from T to obtain the total score. A (+) score indicates a traditional orientation, A (−) score indicates a modern orientation, and A (0) score indicates a perfect traditional-modern balance.

T. M. Inventory

Please express your feeling about each statement below by indicating whether you agree strongly (4), agree mildly (3), disagree mildly (2), or disagree strongly (1).

1. Husbands and wives should share equally in housework.

        4   3   2   1

2. All institutions should follow a democratic process of decision-making.

        4   3   2   1

3. I prefer to live in a small town or a friendly neighborhood where everyone knows each other.

        4   3   2   1

4. Women with children at home should not have a full-time career or job outside of the home.

        4   3   2   1

5. Students should not question the teachings of their teachers or professors.

        4   3   2   1

6. I prefer to live in a large city.

        4   3   2   1

7. Husbands and wives should share equally in child-rearing and child care.

        4   3   2   1

Developed by Manuel Ramirez III and Susanne R. Doell.

8. In industry or government, when two persons are equally qualified, the older person should get the job.

4   3   2   1

9. It's hard to meet and get to know people in cities.

4   3   2   1

10. Women should assume their rightful place in business and in the professions along with men.

4   3   2   1

11. Laws should be obeyed without question.

4   3   2   1

12. You should know your family history so you can pass it on to your children.

4   3   2   1

13. In general, the father should have greater authority than the mother in bringing up children.

4   3   2   1

14. Students should have decision-making power in schools and universities.

4   3   2   1

15. It does not matter to me if my job requires me to move far away from the place where I have my roots.

4   3   2   1

16. Husbands and wives should participate equally in making important family decisions.

4   3   2   1

17. With institutions, the amount of power a person has should not be determined by either age or gender.

4   3   2   1

18. I prefer the excitement of a large city to relaxed living in a small town.

4   3   2   1

19. Children should always be respectful of their parents and older relatives.

4   3   2   1

20. Traditional observances such as church services or graduation ceremonies add meaning to life.

    4   3   2   1

21. Adult children should visit their parents regularly.

    4   3   2   1

22. We should not let concerns about time interfere with our friendships and interactions with others.

    4   3   2   1

23. Children should be taught to be loyal to their families.

    4   3   2   1

24. The biblical version of the creation of the universe should not be taught in schools.

    4   3   2   1

25. Children should be encouraged to be independent of their families at an early age.

    4   3   2   1

26. If you are not careful, people can cause you to waste your time and you will never get anything accomplished.

    4   3   2   1

27. Most traditional ceremonies are outmoded and wasteful of time and money.

    4   3   2   1

28. There is no doubt that the universe was created by a supreme being.

    4   3   2   1

29. Children should be taught to always feel close to their families.

    4   3   2   1

30. We get into such a hurry sometimes that we fail to enjoy life.

    4   3   2   1

31. Everything a person does reflects on her/his family.

    4   3   2   1

32. Eventually, science will explain all the mysteries of life.

    4   3   2   1

33. A person should only be responsible to himself or herself.

        4   3   2   1

34. No matter how many advances we make through science, we will never be able to understand many important things in life.

        4   3   2   1

35. Most religions are primarily folklore and superstition.

        4   3   2   1

36. When making important decisions about my life, I always like to consult members of my family.

        4   3   2   1

37. Religion adds meaning to our mechanized and impersonal lives.

        4   3   2   1

38. If my family does not agree with one of my major life decisions, I go ahead and do what I think is right anyway.

        4   3   2   1

39. Tradition and ritual serve to remind us of the rich history of our institutions and our society.

        4   3   2   1

40. Traditions limit our freedom.

        4   3   2   1

Total T Score = _____
Total M Score = _____
Balance Score = _____

Appendix C

Therapist Cognitive Styles Observation Checklist

Communication Style

Field Sensitive	Field Independent
____1. The therapist does more talking than the client during the session.	____1. The therapist talks less than the client during the session.
____2. The therapist personalizes communications, is self-disclosing.	____2. The therapist remains a "blank screen" for the client.
____3. The therapist uses both verbal and nonverbal modes of communication.	____3. The therapist emphasizes verbal communication.

Interpersonal Relationship Style

Field Sensitive	Field Independent
____1. The therapist is informal and establishes a close personal relationship with the client.	____1. The therapist is formal and maintains "professional" distance.
____2. The therapist focuses on the nature of the therapist-client relationship in therapy.	____2. The therapist emphasizes self-reliance and is problem-focused.

Motivational Styles

Field Sensitive	Field Independent
____1. The therapist gives social rewards to the client.	____1. The therapist emphasizes self rewards.
____2. The therapist emphasizes achievement for others as one of the goals of therapy.	____2. The therapist emphasizes achievement for self.

Therapeutic—Teaching Styles

Field Sensitive	Field Independent
____1. The therapist becomes a model for the client in teaching new behaviors, values, and perspectives.	____1. The therapist uses the discovery approach.
____2. The therapist uses direct interpretation.	____2. The therapist uses reflection, encouraging the client to arrive at his or her own interpretations.
____3. The therapist uses a deductive approach (global-to-specific) to teaching in therapy.	____3. The therapist uses an inductive (specific-to-global) approach to teaching in therapy.

Appendix D

Scoring Procedure for the Bicognitive Orientation to Life Scale

Twelve of the scale items express a field sensitive orientation in the areas of: (a) interpersonal relationships; (b) leadership style; (c) learning style; (d) attitudes toward authority; and (e) interest and natural ability in physical and math sciences versus humanities and social sciences. Twelve corresponding items express a field independent orientation in the same areas of behavior. Subjects express the extent of their agreement with each statement on a four-point Likert scale. Each item is subsequently scored on a scale from 1 to 4, with higher scores indicating greater agreement with the statement. Items 3, 7, 8, 9, 11, 14, 15, 16, 19, 20, 22, and 23 reflect a field independent orientation, while items 1, 2, 4, 5, 6, 10, 12, 13, 17, 18, 21, and 24 reflect a field sensitive preference.

A separate field sensitive and field independent score is obtained for each subject and the bicognitive score is then calculated by taking the absolute difference between the two scores. The closer a respondent's score is to zero, the more bicognitive the respondent is judged to be. The further the score is from zero, the greater the degree of either field independence or field sensitivity.

BOLS

After each statement, indicate whether you: Strongly Agree (SA), Agree (A), Disagree (D), or Strongly Disagree (SD). Please circle your choice.

1. I have always done well in subjects such as history or psychology.

   SA   A   D   SD

2. I prefer parties that include my parents and other family members.

   SA   A   D   SD

3. An individual's primary responsibility is to himself or herself.

   SA   A   D   SD

4. I learn best by working on a problem with others.

   SA   A   D   SD

5. I like a leader who is primarily concerned with the welfare of the group, even if it means that the job takes a little longer.

   SA   A   D   SD

6. When learning something for the first time, I prefer to have someone explain it to me or show me how to do it.

   SA   A   D   SD

7. What my professors or job supervisors think of me is never as important as feeling that I am really making progress in my studies or in my job.

   SA   A   D   SD

Developed by Manuel Ramirez III.

8. Math has always been one of my favorite subjects.

    SA   A   D   SD

9. Some persons do not deserve respect even though they are in positions of authority.

    SA   A   D   SD

10. Whenever I experience some failure or let-down, the encouragement of my family helps me get going again.

    SA   A   D   SD

11. I enjoy living alone more than living with other people.

    SA   A   D   SD

12. I like to get suggestions from others and frequently ask my family for advice.

    SA   A   D   SD

13. It is less important to achieve a goal quickly, than to make sure no one gets their feelings hurt in the process.

    SA   A   D   SD

14. When I look at a mural or large painting, I first see all the little pieces, and then, gradually, I see how they all go together to give a total message.

    SA   A   D   SD

15. I have always done well in courses such as chemistry or physics.

    SA   A   D   SD

16. One of the greatest satisfactions in life is the feeling of having done better than others.

    SA   A   D   SD

17. I learn better from listening to a teacher than from reading a book.

    SA   A   D   SD

18. History and social studies, in general, have always been among my favorite subjects.

    SA   A   D   SD

19. I give people honest criticism even though it might hurt their feelings.

    SA   A   D   SD

20. Getting individuals to compete with one another is the quickest and best way to get results.

       SA   A   D   SD

21. I like to read biographies and autobiographies.

       SA   A   D   SD

22. I prefer to learn things on my own, even if I make repeated mistakes before finally understanding.

       SA   A   D   SD

23. I learn better by reading about something myself than by listening to a teacher lecture about it.

       SA   A   D   SD

24. When I look at a photograph of someone, I am more aware of the total person than of details such as hair color, facial expression, or body type.

       SA   A   D   SD

Total FI Score =   _____
Total FS Score =   _____
Balance or Bicognitive Score =   _____

Appendix E

Client Form for Assessing Diversity Experience

Name _____   Date _____

Rating Effectiveness of Diversity Experience

1. How would you rate the conditions in which the diversity experience was tried?

1	2	3	4	5
Very Negative	Mostly Negative	Some Positive & Some Negative	Mostly Positive	Very Positive

2. How confident were you when you attempted the diversity experience?

1	2	3	4	5
Not at all Confident	Mostly Not Confident	Some Lack of Confidence & Some Confidence	Mostly Confident	Very Confident

3. How receptive was or were the target person(s) or group(s)?

1	2	3	4	5
Very Unreceptive	Mostly Unreceptive	Some Lack of Receptiveness & Some Receptiveness	Mostly Receptive	Very Receptive

4. How closely did you follow the plans?

1	2	3	4	5
Total Improvisation	Mostly Improvised	Some Improvisation & Some Adherence to Plan	Followed Most of Plan	Total Adherence to Plan

Rating Effectiveness of Diversity Experience

5. How successful was the diversity experience in achieving your goal(s)?

1	2	3	4	5
Total Failure	Mostly a Failure	Some Failure & Some Success	Mostly Successful	Very Successful

6. If you feel that you need to change the plan and try another diversity experience of this type, indicate what you think should be done.

Appendix F

Rating Effectiveness of the Script

Name _____   Date _____

1. How would you rate the conditions in which the script was enacted?
1	2	3	4	5
Very Negative	Mostly Negative	Some Positive & Some Negative	Mostly Positive	Very Positive

2. How confident were you when you enacted the script?
1	2	3	4	5
Not at all Confident	Mostly Not Confident	Some Lack of Confidence & Some Confidence	Mostly Confident	Very Confident

3. How receptive was or were the target person(s) or group(s)?
1	2	3	4	5
Very Unreceptive	Mostly Unreceptive	Some Lack of Receptiveness & Some Receptiveness	Mostly Receptive	Very Receptive

4. How closely did you follow the plans for the script?
1	2	3	4	5
Total Improvisation	Mostly Improvised	Some Improvisation & Some Adherence to Plan	Followed Most of Plan	Total Adherence to Plan

5. How successful was the script in achieving your goal(s)?

1	2	3	4	5
Total Failure	Mostly a Failure	Some Failure & Some Success	Mostly Successful	Very Successful

6. How would you change the script to make it more effective?

Appendix G

Client Preferred Cultural Styles Checklist

Traditional	Modern
___ behaves deferentially towards the therapist	___ seeks to establish equal status with therapist
___ expects the therapist to do most of the talking	___ does most of the talking
___ appears shy and self-controlling	___ appears assertive and self-confident
___ is observant of social environment	___ seems to ignore social environment
___ focuses on important others in relating reason(s) for seeking therapy	___ focuses on self in relating reason(s) for seeking therapy

Appendix H

Client Preferred Cognitive Styles Observation Checklist

Field Sensitive	Field Independent
____ self disclosing	____ depersonalizes problems
____ shows interest in personalizing relationship with therapist	____ relationship with therapist secondary to focus on problems to be addressed in therapy
____ indicates that social rewards from therapist will be important to progress	____ indicates that increase in personal well-being will be important to progress
____ global focus and deductive learning style	____ detail-focused and inductive learning style

Appendix I

Figures and Tables Used to Introduce Client to the Cognitive and Cultural Flex Theory

Greater flex in
cognitive and   = Multicultural
cultural styles   orientation to
                    life

Adapts easily to different cultures, groups, and educational and work settings.

Relates effectively to people of different backgrounds.

Holds diverse interests— arts, social sciences, physical sciences, history, politics, etc.

Actively seeks life challenges which involve exposure to diversity—travel, meeting new people, reading, movies, trying out new activities, etc.

Limited flex in
cognitive and   = Monocultural
cultural styles   orientation to
                    life

Limited range of adaptability to different cultures, groups, and educational and work settings.

Relates best to people whose backgrounds are similar to his or her own.

Specialized interests.

Not likely to seek diversity challenges.

FIGURE 1. Relation between Cultural Orientation to Life and
Flexibility of Personality

156

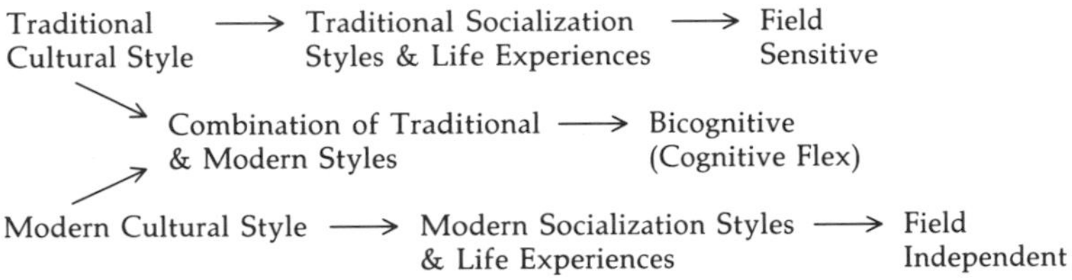

Traditional   ⟶   Traditional Socialization   ⟶   Field
Cultural Style   Styles & Life Experiences   Sensitive

      ↘   Combination of Traditional ⟶ Bicognitive
     ↗   & Modern Styles   (Cognitive Flex)

Modern Cultural Style ⟶ Modern Socialization Styles ⟶ Field
                          & Life Experiences   Independent

FIGURE 2. Relationship between Cultural Style, Socialization-
Life Experiences, and Cognitive Styles

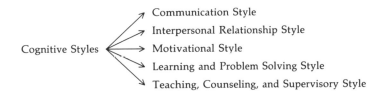

Cognitive Styles ⟨

- Communication Style
- Interpersonal Relationship Style
- Motivational Style
- Learning and Problem Solving Style
- Teaching, Counseling, and Supervisory Style

FIGURE 3. Components of Cognitive Styles

Personality Characteristics of Field Sensitive and Field Independent People

Communications

Field Sensitive	Field Independent
1. Tends to personalize communications by referring to personal life experiences, interests, and feelings.	1. Tends to be impersonal and to-the-point in communications.
2. Tends to focus more on nonverbal than on verbal communication.	2. Tends to focus more on verbal than on nonverbal communication.

Interpersonal Relationships

1. Open and outgoing in social settings.	1. Reserved and cautious in social settings.
2. Presents as warm and informal.	2. Presents as distant and formal.

Motivation

1. Values social rewards that strengthen relationships with important others.	1. Seeks nonsocial rewards.
2. Motivation is related to achievement for others (family, team, ethnic or racial group, etc.).	2. Motivation is related to self-advancement.

Teaching, Parenting, Supervisory and Counseling Relationships

1. Focuses on relationship with student, child, supervisor, or client.	1. Focuses on task or goal.
2. Is informal and self-disclosing.	2. Is formal and private.

Traditional and Modern Cultural Styles

Traditional	Modern
1. Typical of rural communities and poor neighborhoods in urban communities and also of conservative religions.	1. Typical of urban and suburban communities and also of liberal religions.
2. Emphasizes strictness in child rearing and separation of gender roles.	2. Emphasizes egalitarianism in child rearing and in gender role definition.
3. Emphasizes cooperation and group competition.	3. Emphasizes individual competition.
4. Emphasizes lifelong identification with family, community and culture.	4. Emphasizes separation from family and community early in life.
5. Spiritualism emphasized when explaining "mysteries of life."	5. Science emphasized when explaining "mysteries of life."

Appendix J

T. M. Inventory

Name: <u>Imelda M.</u>

Please express your feeling about each statement below by indicating whether you agree strongly (4), agree mildly (3), disagree mildly (2), or disagree strongly (1).

1. Husbands and wives should share equally in housework.

   ④   3   2   1

2. All institutions should follow a democratic process of decision-making.

   4   3   ②   1

3. I prefer to live in a small town or a friendly neighborhood where everyone knows each other.

   4   ③   2   1

4. Women with children at home should not have a full-time career or job outside of the home.

   4   3   2   ①

5. Students should not question the teachings of their teachers or professors.

   4   3   2   ①

6. I prefer to live in a large city.

   4   ③   2   1

Developed by Manuel Ramirez III and Susanne R. Doell.

7. Husbands and wives should share equally in child-rearing and child care.

        ④   3   2   1

8. In industry or government, when two persons are equally qualified, the older person should get the job.

        ④   3   2   1

9. It's hard to meet and get to know people in cities.

        ④   3   2   1

10. Women should assume their rightful place in business and in the professions along with men.

        ④   3   2   1

11. Laws should be obeyed without question.

        ④   3   2   1

12. You should know your family history so you can pass it on to your children.

        ④   3   2   1

13. In general, the father should have greater authority than the mother in bringing up children.

        4   3   2   ①

14. Students should have decision-making power in schools and universities.

        4   ③   2   1

15. It does not matter to me if my job requires me to move far away from the place where I have my roots.

        4   3   2   ①

16. Husbands and wives should participate equally in making important family decisions.

        ④   3   2   1

17. With institutions, the amount of power a person has should not be determined by either age or gender.

        4   ③   2   1

18. I prefer the excitement of a large city to relaxed living in a small town.

        4   3   ②   1

19. Children should always be respectful of their parents and older relatives.

④ 3 2 1

20. Traditional observances such as church services or graduation ceremonies add meaning to life.

④ 3 2 1

21. Adult children should visit their parents regularly.

④ 3 2 1

22. We should not let concerns about time interfere with our friendships and interactions with others.

④ 3 2 1

23. Children should be taught to be loyal to their families.

④ 3 2 1

24. The biblical version of the creation of the universe should not be taught in schools.

4 3 2 ①

25. Children should be encouraged to be independent of their families at an early age.

4 3 2 ①

26. If you are not careful, people can cause you to waste your time and you will never get anything accomplished.

4 3 2 ①

27. Most traditional ceremonies are outmoded and wasteful of time and money.

4 3 2 ①

28. There is no doubt that the universe was created by a supreme being.

④ 3 2 1

29. Children should be taught to always feel close to their families.

④ 3 2 1

30. We get into such a hurry sometimes that we fail to enjoy life.

④ 3 2 1

31. Everything a person does reflects on her/his family.

      ④   3   2   1

32. Eventually, science will explain all the mysteries of life.

      4   3   2   ①

33. A person should only be responsible to himself or herself.

      4   3   2   ①

34. No matter how many advances we make through science, we will never be able to understand many important things in life.

      ④   3   2   1

35. Most religions are primarily folklore and superstition.

      4   3   2   ①

36. When making important decisions about my life, I always like to consult members of my family.

      ④   3   2   1

37. Religion adds meaning to our mechanized and impersonal lives.

      ④   3   2   1

38. If my family does not agree with one of my major life decisions, I go ahead and do what I think is right anyway.

      4   3   ②   1

39. Tradition and ritual serve to remind us of the rich history of our institutions and our society.

      ④   3   2   1

40. Traditions limit our freedom.

      4   3   2   ①

Total T Score = $\underline{+74}$
Total M Score = $\underline{-40}$
Balance Score = $\underline{+34}$

Therapist's Ratings and Notes on Preferred Cultural Styles Observation
Checklist for Imelda: *Initial Session*

Traditional	Notes
_✓_ Behaves deferentially	"Sir" and "Doctor"
_✓_ Expects therapist or counselor to do the talking	Quiet, does not initiate interactions
_✓_ Appears shy and nonassertive	Avoids eye contact, looks at floor
_✓_ Observant of physical and social environments	Said she liked office as she was leaving
_✓_ Focuses on important others when discussing presenting problem(s)	Focuses on relationship with grandparents, parents, teachers, and boyfriend

Modern	Notes
____ Seeks to establish equal status with therapist or counselor	
____ Does most of the talking	
____ Assertive and self-confident	
____ Ignores environment	
____ Focuses on self in discussing presenting problems	

Appendix K

BOLS

Name: <u>Harold H.</u>

After each statement, indicate whether you: Strongly Agree (SA), Agree (A), Disagree (D), or Strongly Disagree (SD). Please circle your choice.

1. I have always done well in subjects such as history or psychology.

    SA   A   (D)   SD

2. I prefer parties that include my parents and other family members.

    SA   A   D   (SD)

3. An individuals primary responsibility is to himself or herself.

    (SA)   A   D   SD

4. I learn best by working on a problem with others.

    SA   A   (D)   SD

5. I like a leader who is primarily concerned with the welfare of the group, even if it means that the job takes a little longer.

    SA   A   (D)   SD

6. When learning something for the first time, I prefer to have someone explain it to me or show me how to do it.

    SA   A   D   (SD)

7. What my professors or job supervisors think of me is never as important as feeling that I am really making progress in my studies or in my job.

    (SA)   A   D   SD

Developed by Manuel Ramirez III.

8. Math has always been one of my favorite subjects.

(SA) A   D   SD

9. Some persons do not deserve respect even though they are in positions of authority.

(SA) A   D   SD

10. Whenever I experience some failure or let-down, the encouragement of my family helps me get going again.

SA   A (D) SD

11. I enjoy living alone more than living with other people.

SA (A) D   SD

12. I like to get suggestions from others and frequently ask my family for advice.

SA   A   D (SD)

13. It is less important to achieve a goal quickly than to make sure no one gets their feelings hurt in the process.

SA   A (D) SD

14. When I look at a mural or large painting, I first see all the little pieces, and then, gradually, I see how they all go together to give a total message.

(SA) A   D   SD

15. I have always done well in courses such as chemistry or physics.

(SA) A   D   SD

16. One of the greatest satisfactions in life is the feeling of having done better than others.

(SA) A   D   SD

17. I learn better from listening to a teacher than from reading a book.

SA   A   D (SD)

18. History and social studies, in general, have always been among my favorite subjects.

SA   A   D (SD)

19. I give people honest criticism even though it might hurt their feelings.

(SA) A   D   SD

20. Getting individuals to compete with one another is the quickest and best way to get results.

        (SA)   A   D   SD

21. I like to read biographies and autobiographies.

        SA   A   (D)   SD

22. I prefer to learn things on my own, even if I make repeated mistakes before finally understanding.

        (SA)   A   D   SD

23. I learn better by reading about something myself than by listening to a teacher lecture about it.

        (SA)   A   D   SD

24. When I look at a photograph of someone, I am more aware of the total person than of details such as hair color, facial expression, or body type.

        SA   A   (D)   SD

Total FI score =   −47
Total FS score =   +19
Balance or Bicognitive Score = −28

Therapist's Ratings and Notes on Preferred Cognitive Styles Observation Checklist for Harold: *Initial Session*

Field Independent	Notes
✓ Depersonalizes presenting problem(s)	Focuses strictly on communication style; no feelings discussed, "business like," no attempt to personalize, "I want to be as effective and efficient as I used to be."
✓ Relationship to therapist is secondary to problem(s)	
✓ Improvement in personal effectiveness is primary concern.	Notes he made on pad were very detailed; goes from specific to global.
✓ Detail-focused and inductive	

Field Sensitive	Notes
✓ Self disclosing	Seems to value close relationships with managers, supervisors, and employees.
___ Personalizes relationship with therapist	
___ Values social rewards	
___ Global focused and deductive	

Appendix L
Family Attitudes Scale

After each statement, indicate whether you: Strongly Agree (SA); Agree (A); Disagree (D); or Strongly Disagree (SD). Please circle your choice.

1. Parents always know what's best for a child.

           SA   A   D   SD

2. A husband should do some of the cooking and house cleaning.

           SA   A   D   SD

3. For a child, the mother should be the most-loved person in existence.

           SA   A   D   SD

4. A child should be taught to be competitive.

           SA   A   D   SD

5. It is all right to have a good time even when there is work to be done.

           SA   A   D   SD

6. People who are older tend to be wiser than young people.

           SA   A   D   SD

7. If a boy's parents do not approve of his girlfriend, he should not go steady with her.

           SA   A   D   SD

8. Girls should not be allowed to play with toys such as soldiers and footballs.

           SA   A   D   SD

9. A child should be taught that he or she is special.

        SA   A   D   SD

10. Children should be taught to question the orders of parents and other authority figures.

        SA   A   D   SD

11. It is more important to respect the father than to love him.

        SA   A   D   SD

12. Boys should not be allowed to play with toys such as dolls and tea sets.

        SA   A   D   SD

13. Men tend to be just as emotional as women.

        SA   A   D   SD

14. It doesn't do any good to try to change the future, because the future is in the hands of God.

        SA   A   D   SD

15. It is all right for a girl to date a boy even if her parents disapprove of him.

        SA   A   D   SD

16. It's all right for a wife to have a job outside the home.

        SA   A   D   SD

17. Uncles, aunts, cousins, and other relatives should always be considered to be more important than friends.

        SA   A   D   SD

18. We must live for today; who knows what tomorrow may bring?

        SA   A   D   SD

19. Young people get rebellious ideas, but as they grow older and wiser they give them up.

        SA   A   D   SD

20. A person should take care of his or her parents when they are old.

        SA   A   D   SD

21. Parents should recognize that a teenage girl needs to be protected more than a teenage boy.

        SA   A   D   SD

22. All adults should be respected.

    SA   A   D   SD

23. The father should be considered to have the most authority.

    SA   A   D   SD

24. Children should not obey their parents if they believe that their parents are wrong.

    SA   A   D   SD

25. Women are just as smart as men.

    SA   A   D   SD

26. It is more important to enjoy the present than to worry about the future.

    SA   A   D   SD

27. The best time in children's lives is when they are completely dependent on their parents.

    SA   A   D   SD

28. A young child should be encouraged to take care of him or herself without asking for help.

    SA   A   D   SD

29. The teachings of religion are the best guide for living a good, moral life.

    SA   A   D   SD

30. We can attain our goals only if it is the will of God that we do so.

    SA   A   D   SD

31. A child should be taught to be ambitious.

    SA   A   D   SD

32. Fathers should always be respected regardless of any personal problems they might have.

    SA   A   D   SD

33. A husband should take over some of the household chores and child-rearing duties if his wife wants to develop her career interests.

    SA   A   D   SD

34. People should be as concerned about their families as they are about themselves.

     SA   A   D   SD

35. A teenage boy needs to be protected just as much as a teenage girl.

     SA   A   D   SD

36. Being born into the right family is as important for achieving success as is hard work.

     SA   A   D   SD

37. A person should be satisfied with what he or she is without always wanting to achieve more.

     SA   A   D   SD

Total Traditionalism Score _____
Total Modernism Score   _____
Balance Score   _____

Most Important Match and Mismatch Incidents of the Week

Name _____

Week of _____

Match

Description of Incident	Date & Time	Situation & Setting	How I Reacted (Include Verbal & Nonverbal Behaviors	How my Partner Reacted (Include Verbal & Nonverbal Behaviors	Describe Areas of Cultural & Cognitive Styles Match	Positive Effects on Relationship

Mismatch

Description of Incident	Date & Time	Situation & Setting	How I Reacted (Include Verbal & Nonverbal Behaviors	How my Partner Reacted (Include Verbal & Nonverbal Behaviors	Describe Areas of Cultural & Cognitive Styles Mismatch	Negative Effects on Relationship

References

Adler, P. S. (1974). Beyond cultural identity: Reflections on cultural and multicultural men. In R. Brislin (Ed.) *Topics in cultural learning* Volume 2. University of Hawaii: East-West Culture Learning Institute.

Almeida, E. & Sanchez, M. E. (1984, September). *Cultural interaction in social change dynamics.* Paper presented at the XXIII International Congress of Psychology, Acapulco, Gro., Mexico.

Beck, A. (1988). *Love is never enough.* New York: Harper & Row.

Beck, A. T. (1976). *Cognitive therapy and the emotional disorders.* New York: International University Press.

Bellah, R. N., Madsen, R., Sullivan, W. M., Swidler, A. & Topton, S. N. (1985) *Habits of the heart: individualism and commitment in American life.* New York: Harper & Row.

Bond, H. M. (1927). "Some exceptional Negro children." *The Crisis, 34,* 257–280.

Brink, T. L. (1984). *The middle class credo: 1,000 all American beliefs.* Saratoga, California: R & E Publishers.

Bulhan, H. A. (1985). *Franz Fanon and the psychology of oppression.* New York: Plenum Publishing.

Buriel, R. (1981). *Acculturation and biculturalism among three generations of Mexican American and Anglo school children.* Unpublished paper. Pomona College.

Castaneda, A. (1984). Traditionalism, modernism and ethnicity. In J. L. Martinez and R. H. Mendoza (Eds.) *Chicano Psychology,* 2nd Ed. New York: Academic Press.

Cohen, R. A. (1969). "Conceptual styles, culture conflict and nonverbal tests of intelligence." *American Anthropologist, 71,* 828–856.

Collins, M. (1954). *Cortez and Montezuma.* New York: Avon Books.

Comaz-Diaz, L., & Griffith, E. E. (Eds.) (1988) *Clinical guidelines in cross-cultural mental health.* New York: Wiley.

Cox, B. G., Macaulay, J., & Ramirez, M. (1982). *New frontiers: A bilingual early learning program.* Chicago: Science Research Associates.

Crevecoeur. J. H. St. J. (1904). *Letters from an American farmer.* New York: Fox Duffield, & Co.

Cubberley, E. P. (1909). *Changing conceptions of education.* Boston: Houghton Mifflin.

Dreikurs, R. (1963). "Individual psychology: The Adlerian point of view." In J. M. Wofsonen and R. W. Heine (Eds.) *Concepts of personality.* Chicago: Aldine.

Ellis, A. (1970). *The essence of rational psychotherapy: A comprehensive approach in treatment.* New York: Institute for Rational Living.

Fanon, F. (1967). *Black skin, white masks.* New York: Grove Press.

Freud, S. (1961). Some psychological consequences of the anatomical distinction between the sexes. In J. Strachey (Ed. and Trans.) *The standard edition of the complete psychological works of Sigmund Freud* (Vol. 19) London: Hogarth Press. (Original work published in 1925).

Garza, R. T., Romero, G. J., Cox, B. G., & Ramirez, M. (1982). Biculturalism, locus of control and leader behavior in ethnically mixed groups. *Journal of Applied Social Psychology, 12*(3), 237–253.

Guthrie, R. V. (1976). *Even the rat was white.* New York: Harper & Row.

Hale-Benson, J. E. (1986). *Black children: Their roots, culture and learning styles.* Baltimore, Maryland: John Hopkins University Press.

Horney, K. (1937). *The neurotic personality of our time.* New York: W. W. Norton.

————. (1950). *Neurosis and human growth.* New York: W. W. Norton.

Katz, P. A., & Taylor, D. A. (Eds.). (1988). *Eliminating racism: Profiles in controversy.* New York: Plenum Publishing.

Levitsky, A., & Perls, F. (1970). The rules and games of Gestalt therapy. In J. Fagan & I. Shepherd (Eds.), *Gestalt therapy now.* New York: Harper & Row.

Malgady, R. G., Rogler, L. H., & Constantino, G. (1987). Ethnocultural and linguistic bias in mental health evaluation of Hispanics. *American Psychologist, 42*(3), 228–234.

Mannoni, O. (1960). Appel de la federation de France. *du FLN, El Moudjahid, 59,* 644–645.

Marin, G. (1975). *La psicologia social en latinoamericana.* Mexico, D. F.: Trillas.

Maslow, A. H. (1954). *Motivation and personality.* New York: Harper & Row.

Montero, M. (1979, July). *Aportes metodologicos de la psicologia social al desarollo de comunidades.* Paper presented at the XVII Congress of the Interamerican Society of Psychology, Lima, Peru.

Panday, A. K., & Panday, A. K. (1985). A study of cognitive styles of urban and rural college students. *Perspectives in Psychological Research 8*(2), 38–43.

Pav Kev, W. M. (1988). *Consciousness-raising: A primer for multicultural counseling.* Springfield, Ill.: Charles C. Thomas.

Pedersen, P. (1988). *A handbook for developing multicultural awareness.* Alexandria, VA.: American Association for Counseling and Development.

Quinn, S. (1987). *A mind of her own: The life of Karen Horney.* New York: Summit.

Ramirez, A. (1972). "Chicano power and interracial group relations." In J. L. Martinez (Ed.), *Chicago psychology.* New York: Academic Press.

Ramirez, M. (1983). *Psychology of the Americas: Mestizo perspectives on personality and mental health.* Elmsford, NY: Pergamon Press.

Ramirez, M. (1987). The impact of culture change and economic stressors on physical and mental health of Mexicans and Mexican Americans. In R. Rodriguez & M. Tolbert Coleman (Eds.), *Mental Health Issues of the Mexican Origin Population in Texas.* Austin, TX: Hogg Foundation for Mental Health.

Ramirez, M., & Castaneda, A. (1974). *Cultural democracy, bicognitive development and education.* New York: Academic Press.

Ramirez, M., & Cox, B. G. (1980). Parenting for multiculturalism: A Mexican-American model. In M. D. Fantini & R. Cardenas (Eds.), *Parenting in a multicultural society*. New York: Longman.

Ramirez, M., Cox, B. G., & Castaneda, A. (1977). *The psychodynamics of biculturalism*. Unpublished technical report to the Office of Naval Research, Arlington, Va.

Ramirez, M., Cox, B. G., Garza, R. T., & Castaneda, A. (1978). *Dimensions of biculturalism in Mexican-American college students*. Unpublished technical report to the Office of Naval Research, Arlington, Va.

Ramirez, M. & Doell, S. R. (1982). The traditionalism-modernism instrument. Unpublished manuscript. University of Texas at Austin.

Ramirez, M., Diaz-Guerrero, R., Hernandez, M., & Iscoe, I. (1982). *How families cope with life stresses: A cross-cultural comparison*. Unpublished manuscript.

Rappaport, J. (1977). *Community psychology: Values, research and action*. New York: Holt, Rinehart & Winston.

Raven, J. C., Court, S., & Raven, J. (1986). *Manual for Raven's Progressive Matrices and Vocabulary Scales*. San Antonio, Texas: The Psychological Corporation.

Rodriguez, R. (1983). *Hunger of memory: The education of Richard Rodriguez*. New York: Bantam.

Ryan, W. (1971). *Blaming the victim*. New York: Random House.

Salazar, J. M. (1981). *Research on applied psychology in Venezuela*. Paper presented at the XVIII Interamerican Congress of Psychology, Dominican Republic, June 1981.

Sanchez, G. I. (1932). "Group differences and Spanish-speaking children—a critical review." *Journal of Applied Psychology, 16*, 549–558.

Snowden, L., & Todman, P. A. (1982). The psychological assessment of Blacks: New and needed developments. In E. E. Jones & S. J. Korchin (Eds.), *Minority Mental Health*. New York: Praeger.

Spanier, G. B. (1976). "Measuring dyadic adjustment: New scales for assessing the quality of marriage and similar dyads." *Journal of Marriage and Family, 38*(1), 15–28.

Stodolsky, S. S. & Lesser, G. S. (1967). "Learning patterns in the disadvantaged." *Harvard Educational Review, 37*(4), 546–593.

Sue, D. W. (1981). *Counseling the culturally different: Theory and practice*. New York: John Wiley & Sons.

Terman, L. M. (1916). *The measurement of intelligence*. Boston: Houghton Mifflin.

Tharakan, P. N. (1987). "The effect of rural and urban upbringing on cognitive styles." *Psychological studies, 32*(2), 119–122.

Torrey, E. F. (1973). *The mind game: Witchdoctors and psychiatrists*. New York: Bantam.

Triandis, H. C. & Lambert, W. W. (Eds.). (1980). *Handbook of cross-cultural psychology*. Boston: Allyn & Bacon.

Varela, J. (1975). Psicologia social aplicada. In G. Marin (Ed.), *La psicologia social en latinoamerica*, Mexico, D. F.: Trillas.

Witkin, H. & Goodenough, D. (1977). "Field dependence and interpersonal behavior." *Psychological Bulletin, 84*, 661–689.

Selected Readings

Angelou, M. (1973). *I Know Why the Caged Bird Sings.* New York: Bantam.

Bellow, S. (1947). *The Victim.* New York: Penguin.

Coles, R. (1968). *The Old Ones of New Mexico.* Albuquerque: University of New Mexico Press.

Ellison, R. (1947). *The Invisible Man.* New York: Vintage.

Fowles, J. (1977). *Daniel Martin.* New York: Signet.

Haley, A. (1964). *The Autobiography of Malcolm X.* New York: Ballantine.

Hong Kingston, M. *The Woman Warrior: A Childhood Among Ghosts.* New York: Vintage International.

Houston, J. W. & Houston, J.D. (1974). *Farwell to Manzanar.* New York: Bantam.

Momaday, N. Scott (1968). *House Made of Dawn.* New York: Perennial.

Quinn, A. (1972). *The Original Sin.* New York: Bantam.

Quinn, Susan (1987). *A Mind of Her Own: The Life of Karen Horney.* New York: Summit.

Ramirez, M., & Castaneda, A. (1974). *Cultural Democracy, Bicognitive Development and Education.* New York: Academic Press.

Rodriquez, R. (1983). *Hunger of Memory: The Education of Richard Rodriquez.* New York: Bantam.

Silko, L. M. (1977). *Ceremony.* New York: Signet.

Ullman, L. (1974). *Changing.* New York: Bantam.

Author Index

Subject Index

About the Author

Manuel Ramirez, III received his Ph.D. in Clinical Psychology from the University of Texas at Austin in 1963. He has taught at California State University at Sacramento, Rice University, Pitzer College of the Claremont Colleges, the University of California at Riverside, and the University of California at Santa Cruz. Dr. Ramirez is presently Professor of Psychology at the University of Texas at Austin, and he is also Clinical Professor of Psychology at the University of Texas Southwestern Medical Center at Dallas, Texas. He has done research and intervention work in Mexico and Puerto Rico and also with Hispanics, Native Americans, and African-Americans in the United States, and has been named Distinguished Minority Researcher by the American Educational Research Association. He is co-author of *Cultural Democracy, Bicognitive Development and Education* published by Academic Press, and is the author of *Psychology of the Americas: Mestizo Perspectives on Personality and Mental Health* published by Pergamon Press.

Psychology Practitioner Guidebooks

Editors
Arnold P. Goldstein, Syracuse University
Leonard Krasner, Stanford University & SUNY at Stony Brook
Sol L. Garfield, Washington University in St. Louis

William L. Golden, E. Thomas Dowd & Fred Friedberg—
HYPNOTHERAPY: A Modern Approach

Patricia Lacks—BEHAVIORAL TREATMENT FOR PERSISTENT INSOMNIA

Arnold P. Goldstein & Harold Keller—AGGRESSIVE BEHAVIOR:
Assessment and Intervention

C. Eugene Walker, Barbara L. Bonner & Keith L. Kaufman—
THE PHYSICALLY AND SEXUALLY ABUSED CHILD: Evaluation
and Treatment

Robert E. Becker, Richard G. Heimberg & Alan S. Bellack—SOCIAL
SKILLS TRAINING TREATMENT FOR DEPRESSION

Richard F. Dangel & Richard A. Polster—TEACHING CHILD
MANAGEMENT SKILLS

Albert Ellis, John F. McInerney, Raymond DiGiuseppe & Raymond J. Yeager—
RATIONAL-EMOTIVE THERAPY WITH ALCOHOLICS AND
SUBSTANCE ABUSERS

Johnny L. Matson & Thomas H. Ollendick—ENHANCING CHILDREN'S
SOCIAL SKILLS: Assessment and Training

Edward B. Blanchard, John E. Martin & Patricia M. Dubbert—NON-DRUG
TREATMENTS FOR ESSENTIAL HYPERTENSION

Samuel M. Turner & Deborah C. Beidel—TREATING OBSESSIVE-
COMPULSIVE DISORDER

Alice W. Pope, Susan M. McHale & W. Edward Craighead—SELF-
ESTEEM ENHANCEMENT WITH CHILDREN AND ADOLESCENTS

Jean E. Rhodes & Leonard A. Jason—PREVENTING SUBSTANCE
ABUSE AMONG CHILDREN AND ADOLESCENTS

Gerald D. Oster, Janice E. Caro, Daniel R. Eagen & Margaret A. Lillo—
ASSESSING ADOLESCENTS

Robin C. Winkler, Dirck W. Brown, Margaret van Keppel & Amy
Blanchard—CLINICAL PRACTICE IN ADOPTION

Roger Poppen—BEHAVIORAL RELAXATION TRAINING AND
ASSESSMENT

Michael D. LeBow—ADULT OBESITY THERAPY

Robert Paul Liberman, Kim T. Mueser & William J. DeRisi —SOCIAL
SKILLS TRAINING FOR PSYCHIATRIC PATIENTS

Johnny L. Matson—TREATING DEPRESSION IN CHILDREN AND
ADOLESCENTS

Sol L. Garfield—THE PRACTICE OF BRIEF PSYCHOTHERAPY

Arnold P. Goldstein, Barry Glick, Mary Jane Irwin, Claudia Pask-McCartney
& Ibrahim Rubama—REDUCING DELINQUENCY: Intervention in
the Community

Albert Ellis, Joyce L. Sichel, Raymond J. Yeager, Dominic J. DiMattia,
& Raymond DiGiuseppe—RATIONAL-EMOTIVE COUPLES THERAPY

Clive R. Hollin—COGNITIVE-BEHAVIORAL INTERVENTIONS WITH
YOUNG OFFENDERS

Margaret P. Korb, Jeffrey Gorrell & Vernon Van De Riet—GESTALT
THERAPY: Practice and Theory, Second Edition

Donald A. Williamson—ASSESSMENT OF EATING DISORDERS:
Obesity, Anorexia, and Bulimia Nervosa